LIFE AT THE EDGE OF THE EMPIRE:
ORAL HISTORIES OF SOVIET KYRGYZSTAN

Edited by
Sam Tranum

Second edition. 2012.

The first edition was published in 2009 in Bishkek, with support from the Andrew W. Mellon Foundation and the American University of Central Asia.

Table of Contents

Introduction 1

The Authors 2

The Interview Subjects 3

The Interviewers 4

Acknowledgements 8

1. The Kulak's Daughter: Umut Aidarova (Kyrgyz, 1932)............9

2. The Veterinarian: Madalbek Keneshov (Kyrgyz, 1928)..........18

3. The Architect: Aleksandr Golovanev (Russian, 1916).............26

4. The Student: Lyudmila Titova (Russian, 1931).......................36

5. The Dancer: Galina Timoshenko (Russian, 1933)....................42

6. The Collector: Roza Shafir (Jewish, 1941)................................53

7. The Officer: Alexander Shafir (Jewish, 1935) 58

8. The Principal: Gafurjon Shakirov (Tajik, 1953).......................64

9. The Favorite Child: Dilrom Ergasheva (Tajik, 1951)...............69

10. The Ladies' Man: Mikhail Bibikov (Russian, 1926)...............74

11. The Party Secretary: Kurman-Ghali Karakeev (Kyrgyz, 1913)....82

12. The Miner: Abidjan Yuldashov (Uzbek, 1935).......................88

13. The Exile: Akram Valiev (Bashkir, 1913)................................93

14. The Teacher: Abdukhapar Bekebaev (Kyrgyz, 1945)............98

15. The Alpinist: Alexander Eropunov (Russian, 1929)...........101

16. The Beet Farmer: Kaliyjan Januzakova (Kyrgyz, 1928)........105

17. The Accountant: Mariya Vysockaya (Russian, 1933)...........109

18. The Deportee: Sofiya Kim (Korean, 1929).....................112

19. The Farmer: Asel Imankulova (Kyrgyz, 1928)..................116

20. The Janitor: Tokon Rakhmanova (Kyrgyz, 1940)................121

21. The Tractor Driver: Ilhomjan Karimov (Uzbek, 1924)..........126

22. The KGB Agent: Komiljan Djurabekov (Uzbek, 1928)...........131

23. The Opium Farmer & Her Husband: Sulayka Arpachiyeva and Karagul Arpachiyev (Kyrgyz, 1951).....................138

24. The Shepherd & His Wife (Kyrgyz, 1931/1932) Dogdurbai Kachikeev and Kashymkan Kachikeeva........................145

25. The Engineer: Joldosh Oskonbaev (Kyrgyz, 1936).............151

26. The Factory Worker: Dilber Ejeke (Kyrgyz, 1941)............160

27. The Kidnapped Bride: Buburakan Muratbekova (Kyrgyz, 1936) ..178

28. The Writer: Sooronbay Jusuyev (Kyrgyz, 1925)...............185

29. The Driver: Pyotr Melenkov (Russian, 1936).................189

30. The Propagandist: Erjigit Shakirov (Kyrgyz, 1931)..........200

31. The Hero: Syinanbyubyu Namatova (Kyrgyz, 1936)............205

32. The Conservative: Oktiabr Akmoldoev (Kyrgyz, 1939).......210

33. The Haji: Abdysh Asanov (Kyrgyz, 1925)....................222

INTRODUCTION

While scholars have spent a great deal of time combing through archives in Moscow, studying how the major events of the Soviet period were experienced by people living in Russia and Eastern Europe, much less of this type of research has been done on Central Asia. But the people of the five former Soviet republics of Central Asia — Kazakhstan, Kyrgyzstan, Tajikistan, Turkmenistan, and Uzbekistan — experienced the Soviet period in distinctly different ways than Russians or Eastern Europeans.

This project was designed to collect and preserve some of their experiences. None of the researchers involved in this project were historians. For that reason, our goal was simply to collect these stories before they were lost forever. We hope that they will be interpreted and analyzed by historians in the future. A searchable version of all the material in this book is available online, to aid researchers looking for information on particular topics.

The stories collected during this project touch on events including: Urkun/World War I; sedentarization; collectivization; World War II; the post-war reconstruction period; Stalin's death; the Khrushchev and Brezhnev eras; independence; and privatization. The interviewees were asked about language, religion, the roles of men and women in society, their school days, their war experiences, migration issues, deported nationalities, agriculture, food, and entertainment.

THE AUTHORS

This book is the result of the work done by the spring 2009 Historical Journalism class at the American University of Central Asia (AUCA) in Bishkek, Kyrgyzstan. It was conceived, organized, and edited by Sam Tranum, who was an Assistant Professor in the Department of Journalism & Mass Communications at AUCA from 2007 to 2009. He has worked as a reporter at newspapers in the U.S. and served as a Peace Corps Volunteer in Turkmenistan from 2004 to 2006. He holds a master's degree in international relations from the University of Chicago, focusing on American foreign policy in Turkmenistan.

The interviews in this book were conducted, transcribed, and translated by 17 AUCA students from Kyrgyzstan, Turkmenistan, and Uzbekistan: Nurshat Ababakirov, Maksat Annamuradov, Abdurahman Aripov, Akylbek Baltabaev, Kseniya Balybina, Dinara Davlembaeva, Gulzara Hayytmuradova, Dovlet Hojamuradov, Rayhon Jonbekova, Nariman Jumayev, Bahtiyar Kurambaev, Nazarbegim Muzaffarova, Maksat Nepesov, Azat Nepesov, Arslan Penjiyev, Dilbar Ruzadorova, and Murat Tuloberdiev.

THE INTERVIEW SUBJECTS

The people interviewed for this project reflect Kyrgyzstan's diversity. They include native-born Kyrgyzstanis and immigrants, Muslims and Christians, farmers and urban professionals, and a range of ethnicities:

The average age of the interview subjects was 75. Most of them — 77 percent—were born before the Soviet Union entered World War II. A few of them — 9 percent — were born before the Soviet Union even existed.

About 57 percent of the interview subjects were men and 43 percent were women. About 51 percent of the interview subjects were Kyrgyz; 20 percent were Russian; 11 percent were Uzbek; 6 percent were Tajik; and 11 percent were other ethnicities.

About half the interview subjects were from rural backgrounds and half were from urban backgrounds.

About 40 percent of our interviews were conducted in Bishkek, Kyrgyzstan's capital and largest city. The remaining 60 percent of the interviews were conducted: in the region around Bishkek; in rural Batken province in the far south; in Osh — Kyrgyzstan's second city, on the edge of the Fergana Valley — and the surrounding area; in the region around alpine Lake Issyk-Kul; and in mountainous Talas, in the western part of the country.

The Interviewers

Nurshat Ababakirov, who is from Osh, Kyrgyzstan, was a senior in the International & Comparative Politics Program at the American University of Central Asia (AUCA) when he traveled to the Osh area to interview Madalbek Keneshov in Kara Sogot and Umut Aidarova in Kotormo. "The children of the interviewees expected somebody older than me to show up and do the interview. Some of them knew me as a kid and they gave me surprised looks, marveling at how fast time goes by and that what they had experienced not so long ago had already become history. When the interview was over, they gave me a new shirt as a gift and thanked me for documenting their parents' words," he recalled.

Maksat Annamuradov, who is from Ashgabat, Turkmenistan, was a junior in the International & Comparative Politics Program at AUCA when he interviewed Alexander Eropunov in Bishkek and traveled to Ak Bashat to interview Kaliyjan Januzakova. "When I went to Ak Bashat with other Turkmen students from the Historical Journalism class, the people there were expecting an official delegation of journalists from Turkmenistan — they had very high expectations and were surprised to learn that we were just students," he recalled. "Their whole families were there to greet us and they were very hospitable, even after they found out we were just students."

Abdurahman Aripov, who is from Andijan, Uzbekistan, was a sophomore in the Department of Journalism & Mass Communications at AUCA when he traveled to the Osh area to interview Ilhomjan Karimov and Komiljan Djurabekov.

Akylbek Baltabaev, who is from Kadamjai, Kyrgyzstan, was a sophomore in the Department of Journalism & Mass Communications at AUCA when he traveled to Kadamjai to interview Pyotr Malenkov and Erjigit Shakirov.

Kseniya Balybina, who is from Bishkek, Kyrgyzstan, was a senior in the Department of Journalism & Mass Communications at AUCA when she interviewed Galina Timoshenko in Bishkek.

Dinara Davlembaeva, who is from Kyrgyzstan, was a senior in the Department of Journalism & Mass Communications at AUCA when she interviewed Mikhail Bibikov in Petrovka and Kurman-Ghali Karakeev in Bishkek.

Gulzara Hayytmuradova, who is from Turkmenabat, Turkmenistan, was a sophomore in the Department of Journalism & Mass Communications at AUCA when she conducted her interviews, along with another interviewer, Dovlet Hojamuradov. They traveled to eastern Kyrgyzstan to interview Sulayka and Karagul Arpachiyev and Dugdurbai and Kashymkan Kachikeev. They also interviewed Joldosh Oskonbaev and Dilber Ejeke in Bishkek.

Dovlet Hojamuradov, who is from Seidi, Turkmenistan, was a junior in the International & Comparative Politics Program at AUCA when he conducted his interviews along with another interviewer, Gulzara Hayytmuradova. They traveled to eastern Kyrgyzstan to interview Sulayka and Karagul Arpachiyev and Dugdurbai and Kashymkan Kachikeeva. They interviewed Joldosh Oskonbaev and Dilber Ejeke in Bishkek.

Rayhon Jonbekova, who is from Khorog, Tajikistan, was a junior in the Department of Journalism & Mass Communications at AUCA when she traveled to Osh and interviewed Abidjan Yuldashov, Akram Valiev, and Abdukhapar Bekebaev. "Before leaving Bishkek, I set up interviews with two old women — sisters. But when I arrived, they canceled their interviews," she recalled. "It was three days before my flight back to Bishkek was scheduled to leave. On the first day, I went out and tried to talk to some people, but none of them spoke Russian and I don't speak Kyrgyz. I had two days left, so I went to the park and to some chaikhanas [teahouses]. Wherever I went, I was looking around for old people. I saw them everywhere, even in my dreams. Luckily, I found three old men: one walking in a park and two playing chess. They were nice and agreed to help me. I felt like I was hunting old people."

Nariman Jumayev, who is from Ashgabat, Turkmenistan, was a sophomore in the Economics Department at AUCA when he interviewed Mariya Vysockaya and Sofiya Kim in Bishkek.

Bahtiyar Kurambaev, who is from Dashagouz, Turkmenistan, was a junior in the Department of Journalism & Mass Communications at AUCA when he interviewed Aleksandr Golovanev and Lyudmila Titova in Bishkek. "The lady I interviewed started taking off my clothes when we were about to start the interview. It was weird in that an 80-year-old woman was taking my coat so that I wouldn't get too warm," he recalled.

Nazarbegim Muzaffarova, who is from Kyrgyzstan, was a sophomore in Department of Journalism & Mass Communications at AUCA when she traveled to the Osh area to interview Gafurjon Shakirov and Dilrom Ergasheva. Although she was staying in Osh, she did her interviews in the village of Uchkurgan, in neighboring Batken province. "I spent an hour interviewing Gafurjon and then realized I had accidentally deleted the interview from my recorder. I was about to cry, but he said: 'Don't worry, come again tomorrow and, now that I know the questions, I will be able to give you a better interview.' So I went back and interviewed him again. But when I returned to Bishkek and connected my recorder to the computer, the first interview was there, so it turned out it hadn't been necessary to go twice," she recalled.

Maksat Nepesov, who is from Ashgabat, Turkmenistan, was

a sophomore in the American Studies Program at AUCA when he interviewed Asel Imankulova and Syinanbyubyu Namatova in the village of Ak Bashat, near Bishkek.

Azat Nepesov, who is from Ashgabat, Turkmenistan, was a sophomore in the American Studies Program at AUCA, when he interviewed Tokon Rakhmanova in the village of Ak Bashat, near Bishkek.

Arslan Penjiyev, who is from Turkmenistan, was a senior in the International & Comparative Politics Program at AUCA when he interviewed Roza and Alexander Shafirat their home in Bishkek. "They were a very interesting and enthusiastic couple," he recalled. "They both had difficult lives and ended up being famous people in Kyrgyzstan. It was a pleasure to interview them and I still keep in touch — they invited me for dinner this week."

Dilbar Ruzadorova, who is from Tajikistan, was a junior in the Department of Journalism & Mass Communications at AUCA when she traveled to western Kyrgyzstan to interview Buburakan Murabekova and interviewed Sooronbay Jusuyev in Bishkek.

Murat Tuloberdiev, who is from Kyrgyzstan, was a student at AUCA when he interviewed Abdysh Asanov in Ken-Aral and Oktiabr Akmodoev in Talas.

Acknowledgements

The project team would like to thank: Eleanora Proyaeva, Dr. John Couper and the Department of Journalism & Mass Communications at the American University of Central Asia, for providing digital voice recorders and cameras; Dr. Okon Akiba and the Student Intellectual Life Committee at the American University of Central Asia for providing the grant funding that made it possible for the students to travel all over the country to collect interviews; Dr. J. Otto Pohl for sharing his expertise about deported nationalities within the Soviet Union; Lois Kapila for copyediting; Nikolay Shulgin, the American University of Central Asia's Dean of Students, for arranging the printing of the first edition of the book; and Dr. Sheila Fitzpatrick of the University of Chicago, for inspiring the project with her class "Soviet History from the Archives."

1. The Kulak's Daughter

Umut Aidarova was born in 1932 in the village of Kotormo in the Nookat region, near Osh, Kyrgyzstan. "In the early 1920s, our family went through a difficult time ... the Soviet authorities labeled my father an enemy of the people and he was sent to prison in Osh," she recalled. Nurshat Ababakirov interviewed her in Kotormo on April 22, 2009.

I was born in 1932 in the village of Kotormo, in Eski Nookat *rayon* [Old Nookat county], a century after it was settled. Agriculture was the primary occupation for most residents back then — there was only a little bit of trade. Eski Nookat was not on a major trade route until the collapse of the Soviet Union, when it became the only connection between Batken *oblast* [province] and the rest of the country.

Eski Nookat is a large valley, watered by the Kyrgyz Ata River, which originates in the beautiful, snow-capped Ala-Too Mountains. The mountainous skyline surrounding Nookat Valley is particularly beautiful. The jaggedness of the mountains contrasts with the even surface of the valley floor. To the southeast, the rocky, snow-covered mountain peaks touch the sky, their slopes are cloaked in evergreens and their bases are naked hills, criss-crossed by animal trails. To the northwest, brick red hills rise from the valley floor.

This natural fortress has given Eski Nookat residents a distinct identity and a sense of security. The population of Eski Nookat includes local Kyrgyz clans and a large Uzbek minority

— they have lived fairly peacefully for many years. Remarkably, the valley has its own dialects of both Kyrgyz and Uzbek, even though it is only 40 kilometers away from the ancient city of Osh, the epicenter of Kyrgyzstan's primary southern dialects.

The Uzbek minority in Eski Nookat is concentrated around the administrative center. The Kyrgyz population, which lives in the foothills, is chiefly engaged in livestock breeding and agriculture; the Uzbek population, concentrated around the bazaars, is sedentary and focuses on trade, craftsmanship, and agriculture.

Eski Nookat's rich water resources and relatively cool weather make it a favorable location for agriculture. The valley has long been famous for its potatoes, tobacco, and delicious apples — known as *jyldyz alma* [star apples]. In 2003, the administrative center, Nookat, acquired the status of a city, since its population had swollen as trade and industry had developed. These days, agriculture doesn't provide enough employment for the valley's growing population. More and more youth are leaving for bigger cities, looking for better lives.

The village where I was born is located in the southern part of Nookat Valley, close to the snow-capped mountains, which provide water for irrigation and drinking. I spent my entire life in Kotormo, only leaving to visit my relatives and my 11 children — most of whom now live outside of Nookat, in cities like Bishkek.

My father's name was Duisho. Before the 1930s, when the Soviet authorities began collectivization, he was the richest man in our village. He was known for his skills as a craftsman and a farmer. Although he never received any formal education, he was a literate person and he had remarkable math skills. He was well respected and my family was considered *ak sook* [white boned].

In 1916, during the unsafe days known as Urkun[1], he fled with my grandparents to Kashgar. When he returned, he built a big, three-room house on the outskirts of the village. The house, standing at the entrance to the village, had a full view of the Nookat Valley. Nearby, there was a slow, shallow river, which watered our fields. The house was well-furnished, with things like copper jugs, old chests, and carpets. All three rooms had wooden floors, which was a luxury at that time. Unlike so many other families in our village, we did not have to lay down thick layers of blankets, or worse, dried grass, to sleep on. One of the rooms was bigger than the other two, and that's where we would receive the guests who often came to consult my father.

The most enviable thing about the house, though, was the glass windows in every room, which provided grand views. Of course, our house did not come close to looking like a mansion in the modern sense, but it was definitely bigger and higher than the other houses in Kotormo. It contrasted sharply with the poverty of the rest of the village, where few people had more than one or two rooms. Even though I was young, I appreciated my father's efforts to get glass for the windows and to install wooden floors. My father was a good farmer, too. We had nine mares, 10 cows, and about 60 sheep. That was quite a large number of livestock for the area, since the Nookat Valley was better suited to agriculture than stockbreeding.

In the early 1920s, our family went through a difficult time. Although I was not born yet, I have heard enough stories to understand the seriousness of the situation. When the repressions started against the *kulak*s, the Soviet authorities labeled my father an "enemy of the people" and he was sent to prison in Osh. Our house was confiscated and it became a school. Our

---

[1] In 1916, there was an uprising against the Tsarist Russian forces and a mass flight to China after the Russians tried to conscript Central Asians into their army to fight in World War I. Estimates of the Kyrgyz death toll range from 3,000 to 100,000 — or even higher.

kitchen utensils, carpets, and copper jugs were sold in the bazaar and the money went to help establish *kolkhozes* [collective farms]. Our family was left with only those things that could not be sold at the bazaar. We moved to our sheepfold and lived side-by-side with our animals. There were no wooden floors and no windows — just bare walls. Then our livestock was taken away and our sheep became the core of the newly established Kotormo *kolkhoz*'s herd.

After three years, my father was released. Our *kolkhoz* hired him as a shepherd and put him in charge of 350 sheep. He did not like to talk about his days in prison but, while shepherding in the mountains, he would often silently cry, remembering his lost years and his humiliation. When I turned nine, I began to help my father with his work.

Every spring, we would make a two-day trip along the Kyrgyz Ata River to Kara Koi *jailoo*, a beautiful alpine pasture, which had its own *mazar* [a sacred place], rocky mountains, thick forests, and rich grass. As a child, I loved to spend summers at the *jailoo*. The mountain air was so fresh. The sun would shine for only about 10 hours, because of the high mountain skyline. At the *jailoo*, we would stockpile food for the winter. There was an abundance of milk from mares and goats so, throughout the summer, we would make *sarymai* [boiled milk curd], *kurut* [dried, salty yogurt balls], and *kaimak* [sour cream].

Down in the village, summer was unbearably hot and everything was usually still until 4 p.m. or 5 p.m., when the heat subsided. Then people would go to the fields and work until it got dark and nothing could be seen. Even children were expected to help; they, too, went out to the fields to work alongside their elder siblings and their parents. The lazy kids were required to deliver food and tea to the people working in the fields.

Life at the *jailoo* was much more interesting than life down in the village. In the morning, I would wake up long before dawn and help my mother milk the cows and let the animals out so that they would have enough time to reach faraway places with better grass. Calves had to be taken to their mothers for milk and then taken away — this was mainly the children's responsibility. Bringing wood from nearby forests to build fires to boil milk was also one of our jobs. Despite my young age, I took a lot of responsibility. And I grew into a thickset girl of average height.

There were about 30 families living in Kotormo by that time and the *kolkhoze*s were fully functioning by then. There was an effort to eradicate illiteracy. Our house was used as the school until a new school was built. Since there were no Russian teachers and no Kyrgyz people who could speak good Russian, we were taught Kyrgyz using Latin letters. We had only one class, which covered the basics of mathematics and grammar. It included students of all ages — 30-year-olds as well as 15-year-olds. Younger students would giggle at the awkward attempts of grown-ups to solve math problems or write grammar exercises on the blackboard.

Then more misfortune came to our family. My father was caught selling a sheep in the Nookat bazaar. He was taken from the bazaar and sentenced to two years in the prison in Osh. I learned later that some local government officials had ordered him to sell a big sheep so that they could replace it with a smaller one and keep the profit. It took a long time for me to learn what had really happened, since talking publicly about these kinds of things — except for repeating the official version — was taboo. Anyway, my father spent another two years in prison.

For a while we were not allowed to go to school. And my elder brother, Mamaziya, was not allowed to serve in the army. It was a big blow for him, since serving in the army was considered a sacred duty for all men, and young men who did not serve were reproached. He had a stroke and never fully recovered.

When I turned 17, I got married. It was February 17, 1949. I thought I was a little too young for marriage, but I had to agree, because it helped my family financially. My husband was Abakir Aidarov, 22, a hard-working and good-looking young man. He was the oldest man in his family, since his father died in World War II. His family — which consisted of his younger brother, his sister, and his mother — was poor. I realized that I would have to work hard, alongside Abakir, to provide sufficient food for my new family.

Abakir borrowed a goat from someone to slaughter it for the wedding party. It was a modest — but not cheap — feast. At that time hardly anybody was in a position to organize parties at all. Everyone was working for the *kolkhoz* and could barely make ends meet. Abakir bought a lot of flour to make bread and to cook other dishes. He invited relatives and friends from the village. As a wedding present, he gave me a scarf he had bought in Margilon, Uzbekistan.

Abakir was 14 when his father went to war and he — as the oldest man in his family — had been required to take responsibility for his family. Because he was the oldest man in the family, he didn't have to got to war. Still, his situation posed obstacles to his development. He did remarkably well in school and his teachers noticed his ability. The local government was interested in sending young people to study in the cities and Abakir was picked as a candidate to be sent to study in Frunze [Bishkek]. But his mother, fearing that his younger brother, Mamatkan, and sister, Ainisa, would not be able to support the family, didn't want him to go. So, shocking his teachers, he deliberately failed the interview.

In our agricultural society, where physical capacity was the most important asset, Abakir became his family's breadwinner and his mother occupied herself with cooking and other household chores. However, since he was young, adults did not take him seriously when it came to issues like distributing land and food.

Abakir fully understood how harsh life for his family would be if he left — and so he didn't leave. At the same time, he realized the importance of education. So, although he didn't have a chance to get an education himself, he did everything possible to help our 11 children get educated, despite economic difficulties that were not so different from what he had faced in his childhood.

When I joined Abakir's family, they lived in a small mud house, which had many holes in its walls. During the winter, everything outside was covered with snow and hungry sparrows would enter the house through the holes, searching for food and warmth. Then, Abakir and Mamatkan would quickly plug the holes with rags, catch the birds, and cook them. That was the reason they had holes in their walls: they were hungry.

Abakir was conscripted into the army in 1951, when he was 24. He was sent to help rebuild Ashgabat, Turkmenistan, which had been destroyed [in 1948] by a massive earthquake. He returned in 1954 because he had problems with one of his ears. Upon his return, he became a driver, delivering stuff from our *kolkhoz* to the village of Kubasai, near the city of Margilon, Uzbekistan. He did that for about two years.

From the beginning, our *kolkhoz* focused on producing tobacco. Men and women alike worked on the farm, but they had different tasks. Men were largely busy with irrigating, spreading fertilizer, and transporting tobacco leaves. Women's work was just as hard: they weeded the fields, picked tobacco leaves, and bundled them together by running a string through each leaf with a large needle. The work would sometimes last until morning, since it had to be done before the leaves got soft.

We got only 60 days of maternity leave back then. There

was only one nurse, named Mingsuluu, for our whole *kolkhoz* and no hospitals. Women would give birth in their houses and, sometimes, in the tobacco fields. So many newborns would get ill and die. The infant mortality rate was extremely high. Also, famine and hard work in the tobacco fields weakened women's health. As a result, names such as Turdubek and Satybaldy, which symbolized strength, became popular among the villagers. Children given the name Satybaldy, which means "bought one," were given to relatives or grandparents to hide them from illness or death.

In 1968, after I gave birth to my eighth child, the blankets of my children's cradle were stolen right in front of our house. I did not bother to look for them, because I knew that somebody who had no children had stolen them, believing that my blankets would allow them to have kids at last. Everybody in our village knew that none of my children had been seriously ill or died. All of my elder sister Salima's eight children were also healthy.

Because women had to both do the household chores and work on the farm, they needed their children's help in the fields. My children usually started helping me as soon as their backs were strong enough to pick tobacco in the fields and they learned how to use the needle to string the leaves together. So that the women could focus on their work, our *kolkhoz* distributed a cup of milk and a slice of bread for each line of tobacco leaves. At home, we mainly ate *jarma*, a gruel made of barley and buttermilk. During those years, older people did not want to eat potatoes and tomatoes, since they were foreign foods.

For us, May 1 was not only Labor Day, but also the day when each family was given the land it would cultivate that year. In a festive mood, our supervisor, Rahman, who was tall and funny, would organize wrestling matches beyond a small hill, where the men could not see us. The woman who won the match would get some extra land. I wrestled a woman who was much bigger than me. I really wanted the extra land to help support my large family and she couldn't stop laughing while we were wrestling — so I won. In the evening, our group of 15 women would organize singing parties and drink *bozo* [homemade Kyrgyz beer], the only kind of alcohol we had at the time.

In 1975, when I gave birth to my tenth child, whom we named Baktybek, I was given the Hero Mother medal, which guaranteed a number of privileges, such as higher wages and the ability to buy products like food, appliances, and fuel without standing in lines. Even though I had so many children, I spent most of my time working in the tobacco fields, rather than raising them. Fortunately, they were smart enough to take care of each other.

2. The Veterinarian

Madalbek Keneshov, who is Kyrgyz, was born in 1928 in Kara Sogot, a village in southern Kyrgyzstan, near Osh. He spent much of his life working as a veterinarian on a collective farm. Once, he recalls, a "…commission alleged that 400 lambs had died of … disease. They took me to the regional committee bureau and took away my [Communist] Party membership card." Nurshat Ababakirov interviewed him in Kara Sogot on March 15, 2009.

My grandfather, Turdugul, was moderately wealthy. He had five children. My father's name is Kenesh. He lived with my grandfather.

The *basmachi* [Central Asian anti-Russian insurgents] would constantly raid our villages and take livestock away from rich people. My grandfather decided to give my father to the *basmachi* to protect his livestock.

When [the Soviet military leader] Mikhail Frunze brought his army to Central Asia, he took control of Osh and then moved north to Jalal-Abad and Bishkek [subduing the *basmachi*]. Kenesh then returned to his father and began living an ordinary life as a farmer.

In 1932, when my grandfather was in danger of being sent to the *gulag*, my father took him to Kashgar, China. I was four. I cannot remember how long it took us to reach Kashgar. Maybe one month or half a month. We fled on our own — only our family, which included my father, grandfather, mother, sister, two younger brothers, and me. Every family made its own way with its own stuff. Everyone just got on their horses and took off. It was summer.

My grandfather sent my father back to Kyrgyzstan to learn whether things had settled down and my father learned that two of his brothers had been sentenced and the other two had fled to Uzbekistan. In 1932, the Kyzyl Emgek [Red Labor] *sovkhoz* [state-owned farm] of Kara Sogot village was established and my father joined it as a worker.

A law enforcement body under [Mikhail] Frunze recruited him. He worked in the Papan Valley for a merchant named Arzibai, who had recruited him. Arzibai was a Soviet partisan who was working for the MVD. While he was working as a law enforcement officer, my father was sent to China. He was captured there, but released with help from local connections. He returned to Papan and resumed his position.

His father, Turdugul died on his way back from China. I traveled all the way from China with him on his horse. He died when we had just reached Kyrgyzstan and he was drinking tea. I cried until my relatives came and took his body to be buried. Then I stayed with my maternal grandparents. We buried my grandfather in Kara Sogot. At that time, my father was in Kashgar, spying. And I remained in Kara Sogot.

In 1936, when I was eight, I went to the first grade. We studied there with *lepkez*, which were adults aged 30-35. I finished the third grade in that school. I went to the fourth grade in a seven-year school on the Shedrih *sovkhoz* of Boru village. When I was in fifth grade, World War II started. During the war, life was very difficult. Living standards fell. There was no food. We were hungry. I was 12-13 then. At the age of 13, I began to work for the *sovkhoz*. I did many kinds of work: I shepherded, drove carts of wheat, and worked in the fields.

From 1943 until 1946, I worked on the *sovkhoz*. We didn't get salaries — we were glad for the mere fact that they fed us, so we kept working.

There were nine people in our family — I was the oldest child. We didn't have enough food. The money my father, my mother, and I made by working for the *sovkhoz* hardly made ends meet. Food was very expensive. I remember one person was killed for bread. Bread back then was very dark; it was made of corn. We would eat *atala* — a meal made of corn — often, too.

When I was working for the sovkhoz, we were sent to a forest called Kyrkkech to get wood for making tools. There were seven of us. It was a two-day walk. For six days, we had no food. A horse fell from a cliff and died and we tried its meat, but it was no good. On the sixth day, we loaded our cart with wood and started back to the village. On our way, we stopped to rest in the village of Taldyk, where we asked someone to cook a *kazan* [pot] of *atala* for us. He gave us bread. At last, something was inside our stomachs. I felt like we had survived a famine. I could not forget this.

When I was young, I wondered if I would ever have a day when I would sleep until seven in the morning. We didn't have tractors. We walked everywhere, even to Osh, where we bought food and clothes. We would stay the night there and return the next day. There were wolves on the way and some people were eaten. The distance between Kara Sogot and Osh is 25-30 kilometers. Once, my father gave me three kilograms of flour, two kilograms of rice, and two loaves of bread and sent me home to Kara Sogot. He stayed in Osh. On my way back to the village on my donkey, I was robbed by starving people. I didn't know them. I cried — I was hungry, too.

We used to work in the fields for days, plowing the land,

without going home. One day we were ordered to return to the village. When we got there, we saw the whole village was celebrating the end of the war. A couple of sheep were slaughtered and cooked. I still cannot forget how our stomachs were full for the first time after long years of starvation [interview subject laughs].

In 1946, after the war was over, I became an *uchetchik*, an inspector of *sovkhoz* issues. I got married in 1948, when I was 20. We dated for a certain period of time and then ran away from our village to Hodjabad, Uzbekistan, near Andijan. My wife's parents did not want to give their daughter to me, because they said my father was poor. We got married in the traditional way in Hodjabad, by a *mullah*. This Uzbek *mullah* did not want to give us his blessing, demanding that we first register our marriage with the government. Islam was strictly controlled back then. In order to get the *mullah*'s approval, we had to secretly return to Osh to get a marriage-registration certificate. Then we lived in Hodjabad for six months before returning home. We lived for 50 years together. She gave birth to nine children. Three of them died. Now I have three daughters — Tajikan, Uulbu, and Maksat — and three sons: Abdymalik, Ulukbek, and Umutbek. I am a happy man, since I didn't have any problems with my children.

In 1951, I was conscripted into the army. I was sent to the Moscow area for three years. At that point, I already had a good command of Russian, since I had worked with Russian workers on my *sovkhoz*. My Russian improved even more in the army. I was a *samouchka*: I studied Russian intensively on my own. In my unit, I was the only Kyrgyz among 40 Russians. They would slaughter pigs and cook them for us. There was a lieutenant named Kravchenko who was the commander of our group. When we were eating once, he moved a pig's head toward me, suggesting that I eat it. Its nose was looking at me. I moved it back in front of him.

My action angered him. He asked, "Why don't you respect me?" I said I couldn't eat pork while looking at a pig's head. He asked, "How come? What do you eat at home?" I said, "I eat mutton." He got angry and said I was a Nazi. I said, "I just cannot eat pork! I cannot! What can I do if pork does not trigger my appetite? Enough! It makes me puke!" Then he asked why I was drinking soup made from pork, then. I said I didn't want to die of starvation. My commander didn't say anything after that.

In the army, I was appointed clerk of my platoon. At that time, mostly illiterate males would go into the army, but my handwriting was good. The colonel of my platoon enrolled me in a special Russian-language training course. After that, I began to feel confident enough to engage in verbal skirmishes with Russian soldiers. If it were not for my Russian co-workers on the *sovkhoz* who used to use sophisticated words and terminology, my command of Russian would not have been so good. Although my grammar was not good, I could use clear and intelligible words. Russians were often astonished.

Then I was appointed *zavsklad* [assistant warehouse clerk]. It was fun. I would send home various stuff. I would feed Kyrgyz soldiers who were hungry and I would asked them for favors. I was 22 years old, whereas most of the others were 19. When I came back [to Kyrgyzstan] in 1954, I worked as a chief shepherd for five years. Then, through the local *raicom* [regional committee], I entered school in Bishkek. I studied for three years to become a veterinarian. Meanwhile, my family stayed in the village. My two younger brothers, Kalybek and Abdildabek, were drafted into the army after me. They served in Moscow and Finland.

I worked on the *sovkhoz* from the time I was 13 until I became a pensioner. I spent three years in the army and I spent three years at the party college. Aside from those six years, I spent my whole life working on the *sovkhoz*. It was an excellent *sovkhoz*: it received diplomas, honor certificates, cash bonuses, medals, and so on. It raised *polutonkoronnyi kurduchnyi* sheep, then *tonkoronnyi* sheep, and then *meronosets* sheep — this last was a special breed that was lost when the Soviet system collapsed. I was awarded the status of veteran of war for working on the *sovkhoz* during the war. I was also given the Chaban Kirgiziyi [Shepherd of Kyrgyzstan] medal. I became a member of the village council nine times.

Once, the Second Secretary of the *oblast* [province] committee came to inspect our *sovkhoz*. At that time, some young lambs had contracted a disease that was affecting their mouths and throats. While inspecting the sheep, the secretary noticed some sick lambs. He was also a veterinarian. He asked why I was not treating the lambs. "This disease is contagious and it is spreading to our veterinarians. They say they are ill too," I told him. "Then why aren't you infected yet?" he asked. "Because I am old. My bones have already gotten hard. If I were young like you, I would contract the disease," I replied.

He left our village immediately. The same day, he organized a commission and came back to our *sovkhoz* to investigate the matter. The commission alleged that 400 lambs had died of the disease. They took me to the regional committee's office and took away my Party membership card. My conversations with the law enforcement officers were tough. I was not allowed to defend myself. They asked questions and I could only say yes or no. Still, I was able to provide clear evidence that this disease was spreading because the sheep had not had enough fodder, the sheepfolds had not been warm, and the roofs had been leaking. When the case was thoroughly investigated, I was acquitted and regained my Party membership. The Second Secretary was found guilty of libel. He was stripped of his Party membership.

Nevertheless, I was well respected among the local Party representatives. Most of them were Russians. Once, I invited our *sovkhoz* director, the head of the *oblast* [province] executive committee, and the head of the regional agricultural committee for dinner. My wife made them soup. We sat outside and, while we were eating, a fly fell into the soup of the head of the *oblast* [province] agricultural committee, Viktor Handyukov. He took the fly out and kept happily eating his soup, whereas the head of the regional executive committee would not even finish his *kumys* [fermented mare's milk] and soup. Victor Handyukov was a good man. He was a good farming specialist and he was accustomed to our culture and traditions.

During the Soviet period, religion was discredited. Mosques were destroyed. There was no large-scale religious observance, but some people would clandestinely practice Islam. I prayed as well. Religious practices were strictly limited; they were considered private, family affairs. Even at *tois* [wedding parties], religious practices were avoided. Popular Muslim holidays were not celebrated on a large scale. Our village didn't have a mosque. The only mosque was in the city. You would go to Osh for Friday prayers, which was allowed. Circumcisions were practiced in secret. Islamic teachings took place within families. You would have to make an agreement with a local *moldo* [*mullah*] to arrange religious teachings for your children. Those who openly practiced religion were sentenced. Nevertheless, people in general didn't abandon religion and, these days, religious holidays are widely celebrated.

Back then, relations between sons and fathers were respected. Moral values were strictly upheld. Muslims didn't abandon their moral values. There was a feeling of general support and cohesion within our community. For the health of the family, there should be respect between fathers and sons, husbands and wives. There is one president in a country, and, likewise, there should be one ruler in the family. Every member of the family should listen to the head of the family. Back then, women had relatively limited freedom. Unlike the female labor migrants today, back then, women were not allowed to live abroad for years at a time. Women's rights have expanded to a great extent. In many families today, women have the dominant role. The current system allows freedom we never saw in our time.

I have three sons and three daughters. They all have higher education. I have 24 grandchildren and nine great-grandchildren. The government is doing everything it can for the youth. The root problem is that young generation does not get proper moral education because so many parents leave the country to work. Unemployment is the main reason they are leaving for Russia and other foreign countries.

Labor migrants will not have a good life, despite their efforts. What one needs for a better life is to build a foundation. One must plant trees and fertilize land. A person should work for himself. [A labor migrant] will bring money home this year, but what about next year? He will buy a car, but it will get old and will need repairs. He will buy a house, but it will not earn money. Everything he earns will be gone in one or two years. Then he will have to sell his car and house for money to live on. At the end, he will be in the same position he was in before he went abroad. Elderly people must teach the younger generation. As our fathers would tell us: "put the words of elders into your bag."

3. The Architect

Aleksandr Golovanev, who is Russian, was born in 1916 and grew up in Bishkek, Kyrgyzstan. Orphaned at an early age, he was wounded fighting in World War II and taken prisoner. "They divided us up in order to kill us. The Germans shot people in the head with their rifles," he recalled. After making his way back to Bishkek, he worked as an architect, designing government buildings. Bahtiyar Kurambaev interviewed him in his apartment in Bishkek on February 20, 2009.

I was born in Almaty but my parents lived here [in Bishkek]. My parents went [to Almaty] so that my mother could give birth to me there. Then, after a month, we returned to Bishkek. This was in 1916. My memories are a little hazy but let me start with Bishkek. Back then it was called Pishpek.

I think I'm one of the last [living] people to have known old Pishpek, which was renamed Frunze in 1926 in honor of the Soviet military commander Mikhail Frunze [and was renamed Bishkek after the fall of the Soviet Union]. I spent my childhood in this city.

In those days, the city had little in common with the present Bishkek: there were poor wattle-and-daub houses everywhere and narrow curved streets. People used to take water directly from irrigation ditches, called *aryk*s. After sunset, everything was plunged into darkness. Only Dubovy Park, founded in 1898, was surrounded by several kerosene lamps and, from somewhere inside it, you could hear the sound of the generator that produced energy for the city's only Edison cinema.

I regret that the present generation will never have the opportunity to see this beautiful panorama around the city: everywhere you could see blooming snowdrops, irises, and different colored tulips. On the streets there were giant poplars, elms, apple and cherry trees, birches, white acacia trees, big oaks, and English elms protecting residents from the scorching sunlight. They shaded almost all of the buildings. It was like a huge, beautiful garden, where you could hear nightingales' warbling and the calls of pheasants.

In the center of the city, there were only a few buildings made of wood and bricks and two churches: St. Nicholas and Serafimov. The names of streets revealed a lot about the lifestyles of their residents. At Klychevaya Street [now Manas Street] there used to be a large number of springs flowing from under the ground. At Kupecheskaya Street [now Chui Avenue] there used to be lots of shops. Doctors used to live on Lazaretnaya [Moscow] and Bolnichnaya [Logvinenko] streets. Zapadnaya [Turusbekova], Yuzhnaya [Bokonbaeva] Tokmak [Frunze], and Atbashy [Molodaya Gvardiya] streets were full of cargo-hauling carriages and teams of carriers.

Now, everyone knows that two rivers flow through Bishkek: the Alamedin and the Ala-Archa. However, in those days there were four. Today there is no Bazarnaya and no Klyuchevaya — they disappeared forever.

There were pedagogical, agricultural, medical, and vocational schools. There were only two drug stores. Where the modern nine-story building with the Ocean [fish] shop on the ground floor now stands [near the intersection of Chui Ave. and Manas St.], there used to be a shop owned by a Dungan, and instead of Molodaya Gvardiya Boulevard, there was a pasture for grazing cattle. The city's Botanical Garden is located on the place where the people who died in the famine of 1932-33[2] were buried.

In those years, we didn't have any railroads. The city had very few stores. The population was about 25,000. In 1925, a

---

[2] The famine that followed the Soviet collectivization of agriculture and killed millions of Soviet citizens, particularly in Ukraine and Kazakhstan.

railway was constructed by Lenin's decree. The Pishpek railway station was located right in the steppe. A Czech visitor came to Pishpek. His name was Intrigov and he came to help build the railway. As soon as the railway appeared here, the city gradually began developing.

The parks started to appear on Chui Street. The Kajovniy Number Two factory was built. At that time, the city was only between [the current] Togtogul and Djerjinsky streets. International workers came to construct the city, including the factories. Until the construction of the various factories, people were busy raising cattle. After 1925, working people were attracted to the city. The city developed along with its industries. Accordingly, the people changed. New people and new industries started appearing.

At the beginning of 1930 or, I think, 1929, construction began on the capital buildings. By 1930, the Medical Academy began to appear on Logvinenko Street. Then construction of a theater began. It was the ballet and opera theater. When the war started, construction of the theater was stopped. After the war, construction was started again. Then a construction boom began.

By the 1950s, Ala-Too Square [the city's main square] had been built. Basically, the city was built during the 1950s, including the administrative buildings, hospitals and the resorts out at Lake Issyk-Kul [about three hours east of Bishkek]. Everything was [constructed] between 1950-1980. It was a grandiose construction period. However, construction stopped when the Soviet Union collapsed in the 1990s because there were no construction materials and no financing was available for construction. Now, not much construction is going on. Most of the buildings you see now were built during the Soviet Union.

When I was eight, I lost my parents. I was left with only an older sister. I was taken to an orphanage named after Krupskiy.

Everyone worked there and everyone studied at a school named after Tashmanov. Everyone was equal. The kids were involved in agricultural activities. Basically, they were feeding themselves.

When I was at the orphanage, it was difficult and we all worked. I started to do dangerous roofing work. Like many poor people, I worked hard for the Dungans in the rice fields for a piece of bread and in the sugar beet fields around Kant for stew made from beet greens.

Once, I remember, two people came to us to pick some of us for work. Guess what? They wanted kids without parents. It was in case something undesirable happened — such as if the child died due to heavy work or an accident — then there would be no one to hold those people responsible for the child's death.

"Do you have a dad?" they asked.

"No."

"Do you have a mom?"

"Yes."

"Not you."

"Do you have a mom?"

"No."

"And do you have a dad?"

"No."

"Then come with us."

It was like this. They did not pick children with one or both parents. I realized then that they chose kids without parents because the work was dangerous.

After some time, my older sister took me away from there. After I left the orphanage, I went to study. I started school when I was about eight. When I studied, there were only three schools in Pishpek [Bishkek]. They were: Tashmanov, Maslanov, and one more school. I can't remember the name of the third school. Schools were not numbered then [as they are now] but had particular names.

The director of the school was Tashmanov and the school was named after him. We only had four teachers at the school. We studied math, Russian, military training, and I think we also had history. The other subjects we studied were physics, chemistry and a foreign language — the foreign language was German.

The teachers were great. The students were also good and we got along well. Tashmanov school was located in Leninskiy *rayon*. Maslanov was located where the Bishkek city hall is now. The current Seytek Center was a school at that time, too. It was a one-story school. Another small school was located at Kalinin. What I remember is that there was no city beyond Togolok Moldo Street — Panfilov Street. Beyond that, there was no city, just nothing. There was a sort of airport, which is now a hospital.

I have three brothers. Two of my younger brothers served in the military. I got a postponement until 1945 because I did not meet the minimom weight requirement. But I felt uncomfortable in front of my brothers. Why do I have to be here while they are serving? I asked myself.

Once, in 1940, I learned that in the evening, a group of young people were leaving to serve in the army. After work, I immediately went there [to the military office]. The military office was where the White House[3] is now. It used to be a one-story building.

I talked to a lieutenant. He asked what was going on, as if

---

[3] As in the United States, the executive mansion in Kyrgyzstan is a big white building and is known as the White House.

demanding to know what I was doing there. I said that I wanted to join the military. Guess what? That day one young man [who was supposed to leave for the army] was missing. I guess he was the only one to escape, out of 40 young people. They [the military office officials] were glad I was there. I went through a medical examination. I was okay for military service. They told me that I should come with my things the next morning. I went home and I told my sister that I was leaving for the army. She asked me how it was possible. She reminded me that I had a postponement.

I went to Saratov [Russia] with a friend for tank training school. I was assigned to a tank unit. I learned about tanks. I knew the BT-7 well and I even repaired them. My service went fine. Conditions were good. Discipline was excellent. We did not have any birthdays in the military unit. We treated each other equally — even other guys from other military units. We never had scandals. On June 15, 1941, the war started.

We heard that in the Baltics, the war was raging. Then we were sent to the Baltics and everybody was saying that there were Germans. We came to a place where the Germans were bombing. We had a car and the driver was killed by the German bombs. When they bombed everything in the city with airplanes, we thought that everybody was going to die.

One day, we were getting closer to the Baltics and on the way there was a small German military unit. We saw them and decided among ourselves to attack them with grenades. We worked out tactics for how to attack them and where to throw the grenades and all that stuff. We attacked and destroyed them. We took their food and all their weapons.

Later, we arrived in Belarus. Basically, we were moving at night. June, July, August, September and October. It was freezing. We moved further, probably to Prague or something. On the way, there were houses with dogs. We approached one of the houses. We didn't know who lived there. We asked if we could rest and have something to eat. I cooked some potatoes.

We only moved at night and only after careful scouting. One day, Germans saw us or found out about us and attacked us. I was wounded. I still have the scar. I fell down and lost consciousness. I lost some of my vision: my left eye does not function properly. The guys from my unit carried me, despite my wounds. I asked them to leave me, but they did not.

The house where we had stayed and eaten earlier — our guys left me at that house and said that if anyone from the house told anyone about the wounded Russian soldier, then he or she would be killed and the house will be destroyed and all the family members, too. "We will come back for him," one of our guys told the owner of the house.

The owner of the house gave me some food. I slept most of the time. I was in pain all the time. One day a German officer, a doctor, came to the house to give a woman an injection. The woman started screaming, saying that there was a Russian in her house. She was shouting that the Russian officer should be shot. But the German doctor was wonderful — just a good human being. He shouted at her in German and she gave me some bread.

Gradually, I became better and better. One day, the woman took me somewhere. I started worrying but then we came to a place where there were about 15 Soviet soldiers. Among them, there were Russians, Kyrgyz, Ukrainians, and others. They fed us some soup. We were taken to a village. I do not remember the name. There was a temporary [German] camp. I was placed in that camp. It was cold. It was in October. We had nothing to warm ourselves with. No blankets. It was like keeping a dog. They treated us like that. No humanity. Nothing. They [the Germans] placed us on a train and sent us to other military units. I said once to all the guys, "Let's run away." We tried but it was unsuccessful.

One day, they brought us into a barracks. There were guards in front of us, behind us, on the left and on the right. They were all around us so that we would not be able to run away. I was walking behind a German. It was cold. I couldn't carry on walking because one of my shoelaces came untied. I fell behind. The German man noticed and came to me. And he spoke Russian. "What happened?" he asked.

Gradually, we started talking. He said that his name was Witsurin. He said that he listened to the radio about the Soviet Union. He said he often listened to Soviet radio and he added that there were some good radio speakers from the Soviet Union. I always like listening, he said. He said that he listened at night or even at 1 a.m. He might have thought that I was a spy or something. He was wondering who I was.

About two or three days after we met each other I was called. We had numbers so we could be called. I was placed into another unit. The group had about 30 people. It was a death row of people. I was in it. Dogs were everywhere. They divided us up in order to kill us. Germans shot people in the head with their rifles. Most of us died.

Then, one day at about 2 p.m. they gathered us all together again — those who were still alive. I looked at them. One of them was Witsurin. He saw me. He took my hands. He told me that everything was all right. Then the Germans released all the dogs from their ropes. The dogs bit people. And then he not only saved me but also he took me to work in the kitchen. I became a cook. I cleaned the potatoes.

One night, Witsurin brought an old bicycle and took me to nearby areas just to show me so that if I ran away, I would know how to get away from the camp. He showed me the homes he himself frequently visited. He gave me hope. It was January of 1944.

Polish hostages appeared in our camp. The Germans

brought them because the Germans had bombed Poland. All of them were against the Germans. But, before they brought them [the Poles], they took all the Russians and sent them somewhere else. I was the only Russian left in the camp.

Then one day he [Witsurin] said that we should go. I completely trusted him by that time. By that time, if the Germans had found out about his actions, he would have been shot. Witsurin took me to Hanover. I remember the house, the workshop. I could even draw the place now if I could still see well. I was placed in the workshop with two Belgian hostages. Next to me, there was a high wall, behind which were Germans. There was a camp next to us. There were two barracks full of [Russian] military hostages there. They worked at a weapons factory.

I worked and worked in the workshop. Once, I convinced the owner of the workshop to allow me to sleep in the camp with the Russian hostages. He talked to the security guards so that I would be able to do it. There was a minibus close to the wall. I told the Russians that we should move it closer to the wall. They asked me why. I said that, if there was bombing, people would be able to escape over the wall. They would not hurt themselves because the minibus would help them jump over.

That's exactly what we did. One day some planes flew over us. They were American airplanes. They dropped bombs. We were wondering why the American airplanes didn't bomb the weapons factory. We thought they were fools. There was a smokestack between the barracks and the weapons factory. I suggested to the others to signal to the Americans that there was a weapons factory. I asked them who knew the best way to signal. We took a headlight from the minibus and connected it to a car engine. Then we pointed it at the smokestack. The headlight flashes were signals and the Americans saw them and bombed the factory. The fourth plane saw it. The

Americans bombed and destroyed the factory. They did not hit us, since we were a little way away, but a part of our barracks was damaged.

The two Belgian workers suggested that I go to Belgium, because they would guarantee me a house there and a life. I told the Belgian guys that I wanted to go closer to the front. They gave me a bicycle. I looked around and at that moment, the owner of the workshop came by with his tractor. He took me about three or four kilometers out of the city and then wished me good luck.

[After the war, Golovanev returned to Bishkek and became an architect].

I was the chief architect for the government for over 20 years. I designed numerous buildings not only in the city of Bishkek but also all around the country. I designed the Technical School in Kara Balta, the Finance and Economics College in Bishkek, the National Bank, the building that currently houses the Ministry of Foreign Affairs, and the Ministry of Culture.

I designed the building for the Ministry of Finance, the main square in the city of Naryn, the Manas Movie Theater, and the technical school in the city of Tokmok. I designed Kyrgyz National University with its kitchen for 500 students and dormitory for 800 students. I have many pictures and designs. I even designed this apartment building that I'm living in.

There was a time when we worked and designed plans all night and day and there were times when we had no days off. It was painful. Now, construction is for commercial purposes only, but at that time people built for the people.

4. The Student

Lyudmila Titova, a Russian, was born in 1931, in Nalchik, the capital of the Kabardino-Balkar Autonomous SSR, in the North Caucasus. Her family moved to the Buryat-Mongol ASSR when she was a child. After her father returned from fighting in World War II, he moved the family to Bishkek, where Titova grew up. "In those years, religion was prohibited by the government ... My mom secretly baptized me," she recalls. Bahtiyar Kurambaev interviewed her in Bishkek on February 26, 2009.

My father worked for the Kabardino-Balkar Bahti Stroy electric station. He was promoted to head electrician. At that time, Chechnya and Kabardinskaya were fighting. And once someone came, I don't remember who it was, and they planned to check how the new station's construction was going, next to the Baksan River. There were spies and enemies all around. And once they cut the main electric lines that brought power to all of Nalchik. The cable was fixed, but it happened again. After that my dad was told to leave the city and we moved to Mongolia [the Buryat-Mongol ASSR].

I studied at the school in Ulan-Ude [the capital of the Buryat-Mongol ASSR]. At that time, there were only seven grades in school — as opposed to 10 now. I studied there and I tried hard. It was difficult and cold. We tolerated everything. We did not have books to read or anything to write on. We wrote on newspapers because we did not have notebooks. We had old books and we used to write in them, between the lines. We did not have enough pens — no ink. We listened carefully to our teachers. Then the teachers asked us to explain what we had studied, to see if we had learned it or not. Then the teachers explained again. Memory was important. I still remember my teachers. They were good.

When the war started, I was nine and half years old. I was studying in the second year of secondary school. After serving on the western front, his military unit was sent to the Mongolian border to fight Japan. There, my dad's unit won the war against the Japan. When the war ended, my dad was released from the military service and was sent to the Kyrgyz Republic.

On December 31, 1945, we came to Kyrgyzstan. We unloaded our stuff from the train around midnight. I continued my studies at Secondary School Number 7 for five more years. That's how I completed a 10-year education. Now, kids have everything and do not want to study. Parents are paying for their kids to study but young people do not want to study. We studied despite being hungry and cold and we tried our best.

We were taught — and we believed — that if we studied very hard, the war would end sooner. It depended on our hard work and on our knowledge. That is why we tried very hard so that our parents would come back. We picked fruit for the war and the fruit would go to hospitals for wounded soldiers. Even if the fruit did not reach the front, we were sure that our work would help the soldiers. We thought that our collective work would win the war.

Life was difficult then and we [her family] did not even have electricity. Nothing. I remember that we had only a small room. We did not have anything to heat ourselves with because it was prohibited. We were prohibited from heating ourselves. This was my childhood. Not much happiness or fun. My dad lost four of his brothers during the war. Our parents cried and it affected us even though we did not understand why our parents were crying.

We did not see the war. We didn't have TV in those years. We couldn't even imagine that scientists could be trained who could invent such a thing as a television where images could be seen. Radio, we had. Radios transmitted important information. Radios reported how many more were killed, which city had been saved, how many losses there had been, etc. We listened carefully.

At that time, we did not have textbooks and notebooks. I just listened to my teachers really carefully. That's how I earned good grades, because the teacher explained something and I repeated it. We had exams. We had to pick a ticket, which had two or three questions we had to answer. The teachers were strict with us. It is different now because the teachers are not as strict as when we studied. In my time, when a student failed an exam, then the student had to retake the exam or study the same subject during the next semester. The student also had to study during the summer when others did not study.

We were serious about our classes. We were afraid that — there were Oktryabryat and Pioneer and Komsomolskaya groups — and we were afraid that if we did not study hard, then these groups would not grant us membership. They would not give us the Badge of Lenin. That is why we tried our best and worked very hard. That's the spirit in which we studied. We trusted our government. If you were a bad student, then you could not be in the Pioneer group. This forced us to study hard.

We also wanted to sit in the front row in class. Only the best students were allowed to sit in the front row. But there are no Komsomolskaya, Oktyabryat or Pioneer groups now. Students are not interested in these groups now. Now, students come to class with their mobile phones to show their photos to each other. When we studied, a fly could be heard in class if it flew around. But classes are now full of noise. They [students] shout at older people. How can they do that? It's not good.

Schools back then were the same as now — they started in September and continued until May. We had to walk a long way to school because there was only one in the area. There were very few schools in those years. There were many students, though. There were more than 30 in one class.

We had a Constitution teacher from Leningrad [Russia]. We studied the Soviet Constitution, all the laws, and we had to pass an exam on the Constitution. We had two French teachers and they were husband and wife. They did not speak good Russian. But they left after the war. For some years then, we didn't have a French teacher after they left.

We didn't have any extra-curricular activities in those years. They became available only after the war years: clubs, gatherings, and outings to theaters. We didn't have anything during the war years. What I remember from the war years are hunger and cold. The only entertainment we had was when the neighbor told us stories. Stories were interesting to us back then like television series are to you now. We were always looking forward to the next night when he would tell another story.

When I was a child, religion was a prohibited topic. The older generation was allowed to attend churches and mosques. But young people were not allowed to pray at religious places and we couldn't even think of God or Allah. Now anyone can attend religious institutions and there are a lot of them. When we arrived in Kyrgyzstan, I did not even know that we had churches and mosques here. People kept their religious faith secret.

My mom secretly baptized me. I was scared because I was young. It was on a religious holiday, but I don't remember which one. It was a hot summer day though. My mom said let's go to church and I said okay. She asked me to stay outside the church and then she brought an old grandma and asked me if I wanted to see how children were baptized. We went into the room. Everyone was standing there with babies. A woman asked me if I was there to be baptized and my mom answered yes. I wanted to go, to run away because I was scared other people might find out. But my mom said to me that I shouldn't offend her. And I was baptized. It was 1949.

After school, I worked at the Sokolnoy plant. That's where I met my husband. He was seven years older than me. He was in World War II, but he was released because of health problems. He was wounded. He liked me and I liked him. We got married in 1953 and the next year I had a baby, our only son. Now I have two grandchildren and two great-grandchildren. Life went by so so fast, with so many problems. There were good days and bad days. I've led a pretty normal life.

People concentrated on work at that time. Conveniences weren't available during those years. In 1953, everyone was thinking of work, of earning more. People had consciences. People tried to help each other. People were awarded with certificates and holidays for their hard work. People were awarded with monetary bonuses, too. We tried to work hard to earn those things and we were given thank you notes from our workplaces. Our work was appreciated. We considered ourselves to be the happiest people on earth; we were convinced of that.

I went to a finance and economics institute and graduated from it in 1968. Then I worked at a plant as an accountant. For many years, I worked. I didn't pay attention to myself and it was interesting to test my strength.

We thought our country was the best and that we had no enemies. We thought that we all lived at the same level, that there were no rich or poor, that everyone was equal. But as soon as the [former Soviet] countries became independent, some people became millionaires. People steal from other people now. No one is paying any attention to ordinary people like us. You just wait and hope for things to get better. We expected that communism would happen. But now we have capitalism and even slavery because one person can hire hundreds of people to work in restaurants, plants, or cafes. People now work not for their country but for those people. We, during those years, could get some support from the professional unions if managers mistreated us. Unions protected our rights. But there are no unions like that now.

I buried my husband in 2001 because of a tragic accident. Then I retired and I wanted to pass my knowledge on to others. The first thing I did was to go to an orphanage for the disabled. I taught art there. I worked with mentally and physically disabled children. I knew an artist, Saltanat, and I asked her if she knew any place where I would be able to improve my skills. She suggested that I go to Arabaeva University because it had opened a new art department. Then I rushed there and it was the admissions period. It was July. I asked them if the university would accept me. The admissions committee said that they could not accept me because of my age. I asked them how that could be a problem. They went and checked again and then they accepted my documents. That is how I became a student.

Now, I study art at Arabaeva. I like being a student. It's not easy to be a student at my age, but since I decided to study, it's my responsibility. I don't know if I will live to complete my university degree. But I want to and I will try. I try to be energetic and go to class. I study part-time and I read literature for my classes. I prepare my homework. April and May are the exam months. I don't pay for the university tuition because of my age. My fellow students accept me as an equal and most of my fellow students at the university are people with families. We listen to lectures and talk to each other and exchange phone calls. I do not consider myself an old woman.

5. The Dancer

Galina Timoshenko was born in 1933 in the village of Gryaznuha, near Novosibirsk, Russia. Her father, older brother and older sister died in World War II. Her mother got sick and "the doctors recommended she move to a warm country with a lot of watermelons. So we went to Kirghizia [Kyrgyzstan]." In Bishkek, she met her husband, built a house, worked in a factory, raised her children, and watched the fall of the Soviet Union. Kseniya Balybina interviewed her in Bishkek on February 18, 2009.

My mother, Anastasia Efimovna Timoshenko, was born into a wealthy family. She was the youngest of 17 children. After the revolution, in 1917, my grandparents were dispossessed because they had a mill, they owned a stable with horses and a lot of land. Why they were dispossessed, I still don't understand clearly, because they had no hired workers and they didn't need any because when my mom was born, her older brothers and sisters already had their own families. They all lived together and that is why there was no need to hire people, because they had their own labor force.

My mom told me lots of interesting stories about their preparations for the winter, when they canned a variety of things. I remember that when they made sauerkraut, the smallest children were put in tanks with cabbage and they stomped their feet in there. Also, in the beginning of winter they slaughtered livestock and then the whole family molded enough *pel'menis* [Russian tortellini] for all of them for several months. Then they put these *pel'menis* outside in the cold and then the frozen product was put in bags and put in the barns. We also stored hams, sausages, and other products in barns. Big pieces of ice were cut down on the river and lowered into a cellar, which was like our refrigerator. We stored food products there. The ice in a cellar only thawed at the end of the summer.

When my mother celebrated her sixteenth birthday, she married. Her husband was eight years older then her. He worked as a station inspector. My mother was a lucky woman because this man loved her and took care of her, although he only saw her a few times before the marriage. Their parents had talked about the wedding and decided that my mother should marry the station inspector. It was accepted in society back then that such decisions were made by parents. Two years later, my older sister, Tamara, was born and three years after that, my mother's husband died under a train.

My mother met my father in 1930. My father was Stepan Timoshenko. He was a very handsome Don Cossack. He was a widower, and he had two children: a son, Vasily, who was older, and a daughter, Njura. He hid this from my mom and told her about it only when I was born. His children were brought up in his sister's house at first, but as soon as my mother found out about them, they were brought to live with us. My mother accepted them as her own.

I don't remember my father that well because I was only nine years old when the war began and he and my older brother, Vasily, were taken away from us on the front. In 1942, we received letters about their deaths. One year later, my older step-sister, Njura, also went to the front. Then we received a notice that said she was missing. When I grew up, I searched for her for a long time. I wrote to our village *soviet* in Gryaznuha and to the Novosibirsk city administration but, unfortunately, my search produced no results.

I ran to the railway station every week and waited for my father for more than two years after the war had ended. Many people came back, and I trusted that, in time, my father, too, would get off a train.

Life during the war was hungry; I wanted to eat all the time. It was very difficult for my mother to support my sister Tamara and me, so she attached us to our neighbors and friends, where we took care of their small children, and they fed us a little. I remember an incident from childhood that seems very amusing to me now. My mother's friend Zoe Timofeevna asked me to look after her two-month-old daughter. I often helped them out. Their family had been evacuated from Ukraine and for some reason they always had a lot of bread, although our family could get only one loaf of bread and only with special coupons. One day, Zoe Timofeevna's mom treated me to a sandwich with red caviar. It was considered a luxury and a sign of prosperity. I'd never seen or tried caviar before. And this caviar seemed terrible to me. I brushed it away with my finger onto the table and then ate the bread and butter. I remember my mother's friends were surprised and thought that I wasn't hungry because I didn't eat the caviar.

I went to school in 1939. There was no school in our village and so it was necessary to walk four kilometers every day to the next village. In our village there were seven students, so we gathered together and walked through the pine forest on the way, singing songs so that it would not be boring or scary. I was a good student and I had a very good memory. It's a pity that I was only able to finish five classes because, to continue, I would have had to go to Novosibirsk, which my family could not afford. I remember an incident from my school years: We had a shortage of cloth, so usually we had no extra dresses for school. One day, I sewed a dress from the striped cover of a mattress. It was the most elegant, beautiful dress that I could afford. My teacher, when she saw me in this dress, complimented me on my sewing skill. Later, the school gave me a coupon to get a new dress from Novosibirsk. The new dress was grey and not that nice, but I put red ribbons on it and buttons and it became very beautiful.

At this time, my mother worked as a nurse in a hospital. She had to wash bandages and linens in the Ob River and she chilled her kidneys badly. In 1939, she had to have one kidney removed and the second one started to hurt. The doctors recommended that she move to a warm country with a lot of watermelons. So we went to Kirghizia. It was 1948. Unfortunately, we couldn't bring any photos of my father with us and he remains only in my memory.

My first impression of Frunze [Bishkek] was that it was a clean, green, small town. There, I learned about things like irrigation ditches for the first time in my life; I found that pure water always flowed there. And also, I saw a red apple for the first time in my life. It was so big and beautiful. I had seen such apples only in my ABC book before.

When we arrived in Frunze, my mother got a job in the city hospital as a nurse, and my sister and I went to work in a factory named after Lenin, which made cartridges. Although there were many evacuated factories in the city, there was a real lack of jobs, and it was a big success to get one. I was also accepted into the Komsomol. Every one of us believed in the ideals of communism, everyone tried to work as well as possible and so as not to dishonor our positions as Komsomol members. We often went to Komsomol meetings and community work days.

There were a lot of social activities outside of working hours in those times. We built stadiums, constantly planted new trees, and built kindergartens and houses. We watched the city grow. When we first moved to Frunze, it was a very small town — the present Akhunbaeva Street was its southern border. There were huge fields that stretched from there to the mountains where, in the spring, poppies and tulips flourished. On the north side, it ended at Jibek Jolu Street; on the east side, it ended at Almatinskiy Street; on the west — Bakha Street.

That small town was half the size Bishkek is today. In the centre of the town, where the eternal flame is now, behind the present TsUM building, was a huge market with greens, fruits and vegetables, and the watermelons for which we had moved to the country. I saw watermelons for the first time in my life.

They were very sweet and striped, with big black seeds. It seems to me that watermelons like those can't be found anymore.

My mother, my sister and I lived in a tiny room on the second floor of a building until I got married. The heating system was the oven, the floors were wooden, and in the middle of the room there was a round table covered with a cloth and on this table, in the fashion of that time, there was a decanter of pure water and a glass on a white napkin.

At the Lenin factory, I got acquainted with my future husband, the father of my future children. His name was Anatoly Pavlovich. He worked in the same place as me. He started working at 14 and, since his family lived far from the factory and there was no public transportation, he quite often had to spend the night at the factory. Along with his friends, he got into huge boxes with cardboard cartridge sleeves and slept there. He said it was warm and soft.

When we met, he was 20 years old. When he first started working, he was an apprentice to a turner. He was then promoted and operated a lathe himself. After that, he learned how to repair lathes. I remember he told me that he and his friends, to show that they had already become adults, didn't change their clothes after work and it was considered especially glamorous if there were traces of lubricating oil on their hands so that everybody could see that they worked at the factory.

I met with [dated] Anatoly for two years before we got married. Unlike my mother, I chose my husband by myself. I went with him to Fuchik Park for dances in the summer. They consisted of two, two-hour rounds. Anatoly would buy tickets for both rounds at once so that we could dance all evening long.

I had white canvas shoes and, before the dances I'd polish them with tooth-powder so that they looked snow-white. To avoid getting them dirty, I walked to the park barefoot and then washed my feet in the irrigation ditch and only then put on my shoes. All my girlfriends did the same. Also, I had a fashionable dress with a pleated skirt and short sleeves. We never took any dance lessons, but Anatoly and I always won those dancing evenings — probably, because we liked to dance very much.

In Fuchik Park there was also an open-air theater. Celebrities from all over the Soviet Union came there to perform. Tickets were rare and they weren't cheap, but Anatoly somehow managed to get tickets for every premiere.

On holidays, we had parades and demonstrations on the main square of Frunze [Bishkek], the one that's now called the "old" square, where the parliament, the Jogorku Kenesh is. On the Day of International Solidarity of Workers, May 1, and on the Day of the Great October Socialist Revolution, November 7, all of us gathered near our factory in the early morning. The mood was joyful, people brought accordions and guitars. We had demonstrations with songs and dances. We also held posters with photos of members of the *politburo* and the Supreme Soviet above our heads.

Now I watch TV and I understand that these parades were somehow similar to modern Brazilian carnivals, because each enterprise had its own float on which it showed the results of its work. We carried, for example, cardboard models of the machine tools that were made by our factory. The workers from the fabric factory carried samples of fabrics. Everybody went home after the parade and we loaded our tables with food and people went visiting from house to house until morning. In general, people knew how to celebrate holidays in a good way: they drank a little bit and sang too much. There were no tape players or TVs back then, so we entertained ourselves in the only way we could.

Anatoly and I got married in the autumn of 1954. We lived in a tiny semi-basement room in an old wooden house with his mother. Our house stood at the intersection of Kiev Street and Soviet Street, where the Glavpochtampt [main post office] is now. My oldest son, Boris, was born there.

There were few apartments at that time so the factory would give young families a place and some building materials. On days off, we built our house. It was part of a long, one-story barracks that was divided into 10 separate flats, but we were very glad because it was our first house. We built it quickly. The foundation was laid in the spring of 1959, and in late autumn of the same year we celebrated our house warming. It had two small rooms. In one of them, there was an oven in the corner and nothing else. At our house warming, we got gifts including an iron bed, a table and two stools. We began to grow indoor plants so the place would seem cozy and not so empty. In a big wooden tub in the middle of one of the rooms, we grew a Chinese rose. But, still, there was so much empty space that Boris used to play football there.

Men played dominoes and cards in the evenings, and women had their own interests — we shared patterns for sewing clothes, or for knitting. There was a lack of clothes at that time and the clothes that were available were really expensive, so we made clothes for ourselves and for our children.

I had a daughter, Tamara, in 1960. Our family grew, our responsibilities increased, and the room didn't seem big enough for us anymore. So we had to attach another room. Back then, there was no maternity leave so, two months after Tamara's birth, I had to go back to work. To my pleasure, my mother took care of my children because the nursery only took children starting from three months.

People didn't advertise pregnancy back then. Talking about pregnancy was not accepted. Even relatives only learned that someone was expecting when her stomach was too big to hide anymore. There were no ultrasounds, so nobody knew whether they would have a boy or a girl. So children's clothes were bought only after the child had been born. The choice was not big: blue for boys, pink for girls. And there were long lines for diapers so, basically, we made them ourselves. I only learned about Pampers [disposable diapers] when my first great-grandson was born.

And by the way, there were lines not only for diapers but for food and clothes. And luxury goods, like carpets, washing machines, refrigerators, and TVs — it was possible to buy them only with coupons. These coupons were distributed by various enterprises to their best workers. We, in due time, with coupons, got a carpet and a Kirghizia brand washing machine. We were so happy!

I remember that a TV was a luxury and everyone wanted one. Our neighbors first bought a TV in 1968. It was a small screen before which there was a huge lens on a leg, through which it was possible see something. There were not many channels. Actually, there was only one and it transmitted basically news, feature films, and cartoons for children and sometimes sports — football and hockey. The image was black-and-white, but it was very strange, as if you were looking though a window into another world. All the tenants from about 30 neighboring apartments jammed into one small room in the evenings to watch it.

And we bought a Spidola radio. We listened to the news and learned about everything that was happening in the world and we also listened to new songs. The electricity switched off and on then as often as it does now. So when there was electricity, our radio was never silent. There's no need to talk about street lights — there weren't any. But near us there was Chapaev Park, where every weekend we walked with friends and their children and arranged — as they are now called — picnics.

I worked with my husband, but our combined income wasn't enough for our family and so, when our children went to school, I had to move to another factory— Tyajelectromash, which did heavy electromechanical engineering. I worked there as a press operator, making plastic cases for devices. The work was heavy and harmful, but it paid 300 *ruble*s [a month] and that was much more than my husband earned. Working eight hours a day, he received only 160 *ruble*s [a month]. We tried to earn as much as possible. Once, my photo was published in a local newspaper called Evening Frunze and it named me as the best woman worker of my brigade. I was very proud of it. Now I show this photo to my grandchildren.

After I went to work in the other factory, we could get furniture and anything we needed. Every summer we went to Lake Issyk-Kul to have a rest in a factory boarding house. The family permit for 12 days cost 40 *ruble*s. When the children grew up, my mother and I flew several times to see our relatives who had remained in Novosibirsk. The ticket cost 32 *ruble*s. Now we can only dream about being able to afford that kind of thing.

I never would have guessed that I

would have to remember how to buy products with cards, as we did in the war years. However, Gorbachev came to power in the 90s [sic] when the Soviet Union had collapsed and, in that period, I could afford 300 grams of flour, two bars of soap, a half-kilo of sugar, and two bottles of vodka per month. There was a joke at the time, suggesting that it was necessary to either wash your hands with soap or drink your tea with sugar — because both were expensive and rare.

Nobody drinks vodka in our family, but we always bought it because all deals at the time were conducted not in *rubles*, but in vodka. For example, to repair boots or to buy coal, the payment was a bottle of vodka. And when Gorbachev enacted the "dry law," everyone just began to make *samagon* [moonshine], including me. We had a lot of recipes for *samagon*. We purified it with charcoal, milk, and potassium permanganate and then infused it with cedar, added some vanilla, and got a beverage like cognac. Then payment for all services was a bottle of *samagon*.

Then we suddenly understood that until the fall of the Soviet Union, we had not been building communism, we had been living communism. The state had cared for us, we had been able to look to the future with confidence and plan our lives. We had work and our salaries were sufficient to live on. In 1982, when I retired, my pension was 132 *rubles*. I could provide for myself completely and even save a little bit. Later, my pension became 10,000 *rubles*, but it was impossible to buy anything with them. And after the national currency [of Kyrgyzstan], the *som*, was introduced, one *som* was worth about 20 *rubles* and my first pension payment in *soms* was around 30 *soms*. Here we have such arithmetic!

Coming back to my family, 26 years ago I was widowed — my husband Anatoly died. My eldest son, Boris, was married and his daughter Yulia was one year old. My children realized my dream — to get a higher education. My son finished the

Agricultural Institute, and my daughter — the Polytechnical Institute. My husband and I saw everything in our lives: cold and famine and illiteracy. We tried to give our children everything that we couldn't afford for ourselves.

Now I have three grandchildren and one great-grandson. I have lived a long life. Although there have been many losses, difficulties and problems, I am still the happiest person in the world. I am surrounded by good people, my children and grandchildren take care of me and I remember the past with pleasure. So I have remembered my history and again I have seen myself at dances in polished white shoes, young, and beautiful.

6. THE COLLECTOR

Roza (Henkina) Shafir was born in 1941 in Ukraine. She identifies herself as Jewish, although she says she is an atheist. Her primary language is Russian. She graduated from college with a degree in economics and worked in factories as an administrator until retirement. She and her family moved to Bishkek in 1970. Arslan Penjiyev interviewed her in her apartment in Bishkek on March 19, 2009.

I was born on July 13, 1941, in the city of Dnepropetrovsk, Ukraine. When the war began in the Ukraine, I was evacuated with my mother to Derbent [in the Republic of Dagestan, in Russia]. My father left for the front during the first days of the war and was there until November 1944. In November 1944, my father died, and my mother and I moved to the Moscow area, to the city of Electrostal.

In 1946 we were found by my grandfather (my mother's father) and moved back to Ukraine to the city of Belaya Tserkov [White Church]. I began school there in 1948 and graduated from high school there. The city was very beautiful but, as a result of the war, it was ruined ... almost back to the Stone Age. The reason was that there was an enormous number of military facilities there during the war. Moreover, the city itself was very small and located 38 kilometers from Kiev. Although people back in those days were very friendly — doors were not locked at all —many people did not own property and, like us, rented apartments.

My mother brought me up. She didn't get married a second time. In addition, my grandfather educated me, too.

Everything was so inexpensive in those days, you could get anything for *kopek*s [pennies]! Ice cream — 10 *kopek*s, for a *pirajok* — four *kopek*s, for a soda—three *kopek*s. I tried to earn 10 *kopek*s for ice-cream, so I studied very hard. I also collected portraits of actors. They were like mini-photos with complete information about the actor on the other side.

Once, my mother and I went to the market. At this time many people were coming back from Germany — our soldiers, military men, who were in Germany with their wives — and one of these wives was selling German dolls. And my mother did not buy me anything for dinner that day, but bought me a doll. I named it in honor of my girlfriend — Zojka. This doll was a unique toy in the house, not only for me, but also for my girlfriends. Its head was made of ceramic,  and everything else was made of cloth. Also, she was able to say "mother." It was a very beautiful doll. But, once, one girl asked me if she could play with it and dropped it and it was impossible to fix. I promised myself that when I grew up I would get a new doll, one that could do something like moving, talking, etc. So, every time my friends from abroad come for a visit, they bring me dolls.

After graduation [from high school], I was accepted to the Moscow Financial and Economics Institute. In 1960, I got married to Alexander Lvovich [Shafir]. He was our neighbor — he rented an apartment next door and he had just finished mili-

ple and friends. Even now, we keep in touch with our classmates through the website Odnoklassniki.ru. Recently, we attended a class reunion and it was quite interesting that our teacher recognized me right away. To be honest, that was somewhat strange. Probably, it is because I still have a kind of a youthful look. It is such a pity that time has quickly flown by — really a pity. Trust me, life passes so fast. It seems that just yesterday, you were 20, and today you are 68. Everything has flown by in an instant.

7. THE OFFICER

Alexander Shafir was born in 1935 in Tiraspol, Moldovia. He identifies himself as Jewish, though he says he is not religious. He spent his life as an officer in the Red Army, but always felt that his career was stymied by prejudice. When he had trouble getting into a military academy, his commander explained: "You know why you haven't been accepted? Because you are a Jew." Arslan Penjiyev interviewed him March 12, 2009 in Bishkek.

I was born in the second largest city in Moldova: Tiraspol. Life there was like life everywhere in the Soviet Union. People worked, went to the cinema and believed in a bright future. I was born on February 24, 1935, and my nationality is Jewish —I am a divine person, so to speak. From history, we know that this nation has created three religions — Judaism, Christianity, and Islam. It is a shame that now they are at war with each other. So, I was born in 1935 and there was an interesting thing that happened to me when I turned six. My sister in 1941 was at a Pioneer camp near Odessa [Ukraine]. My mother and I went to Odessa to take her home. We jumped on a train and, at this time, Molotov gave his speech. It was early morning and there was no sign of trouble. I remember that my dad was trying to tell us something through the train window, but we didn't hear a word and just left. As we learned later, the beginning of the war between the Soviet Union and fascist Germany was announced.

So, we arrived in Odessa, but the camp was not releasing children anymore. I don't know the exact reason why, but the children were not allowed to be taken by their own parents. I remember how my mother hid me in a hedge and ran away to get my sister and when she came back holding her, we rushed off to the train station. My mother did not take my sister's clothes or anything.

I remember when we stopped at a relative's house and I was sleeping on a bed with my sister. I was little and my sister was three years older than me. For some reason I remember that that night we heard an alarm, meaning that the Germans had started bombing Odessa. It was the first day of the war June 22.[4]

The radio warned, "Gas!" and my sister closed my mouth and nose so I couldn't breathe. She was also little, but she had already attended second grade and most likely learned somewhere that she was supposed to do that, but I started to choke and pulled away. Anyway, we had to run away again. When we reached Tiraspol and were walking home from the station, I saw a lot of coffins holding military men. They had already bombed and destroyed the city. So quickly-quickly we left for Kharkov [in northeastern Ukraine] and then Kazakhstan — to Petropavlovsk, and then to Kokshetau.

My father was conscripted into the army during the first days of the war. He was killed during the war. He is, by the way, in "the Book of Memory" of Soviet officers. It is a pity that there are no pictures of him left. His name was Lev Markovich [Shafir]. Those were tough times, but we survived.

During the war, I ate turtle soup. We got food like that because my father was at the front. Our daily provisions consisted of turtle soup and two slices of bread. So, my sister took the bread and I ate the turtle soup. Obviously, my sister was not a fan of the turtle soup.

My father's elder brother found us and brought us to

---

[4] This probably refers to Soviet Foreign Minister Vyacheslav Molotov's June 22, 1941, speech to the Soviet people, announcing Germany's invasion of the Soviet Union.

Tashkent and then, after the Germans had been driven away, back to Moscow. My mother got a job in Moscow.

In 1949, I entered a military preparatory school named Stalinskie Spetsy. There I completed the eight, ninth, and tenth grades. Admission to such a school was a very serious thing — there were 11 candidates per spot. After the war, new employees were needed, so the Second Moscow Artillery Preparatory School prepared experts in different areas. If, in Suvorovsky, schools prepared infantry and aircraft personnel, our school prepared artillery men and engineers.

When I was studying in the preparatory school, during my final examinations some supervisors lowered my grades and I understood that my nationality was the reason. I remember how my teachers were trying to help me out in every possible way, but I couldn't get a gold medal even though I studied very well — I graduated from MAPS with a silver medal. The problem was that the board of educators interfered in my academic success.

They were trying to block me in every way possible. For example, when a transfer to Rostov opened up, there were a few Jewish applicants but none of us were accepted. In those times, there were three nationalities that were treated badly: Jews, Germans, and Koreans. Why? Because we were nationalities that had our own states. I guess if the Jewish state had not existed, things would have gone differently. The thing is that the people treated Jews pretty well, unlike the state.

In 1952, I finished preparatory school and transferred to Leningrad. I spent three years there. From the time I was in the ninth grade, I was actively engaged in gymnastics and performed at various all-Union competitions. Well, all military men should be engaged in some kind of sport. I chose gymnastics and when I was studying in Leningrad, I started wrestling and lifting weights, too. I guess that's why I am not tall.

I graduated as a lieutenant in 1955. I had the right to transfer to Germany, but I was refused because of my nationality. I was an outstanding officer and could have been approved for such military business trips. So, in 1955 I was sent to the Kiev district, but from Kiev they sent me to an unknown, little town called Belaya Tserkov. Nevertheless, every cloud has a silver lining — because I met my future wife there.

In 1956, together with some young soldiers, I was sent to cultivate virgin lands in Kazakhstan.[5] Actually, I was recently awarded a special medal called "50 Years of Virgin Soil Cultivation." At a ceremony at the Kazakh Embassy in Kyrgyzstan, I was the only Kyrgyz citizen awarded this medal. During the 1950s, I worked in the Kustanay area of the Kazakh Soviet Socialist Republic. That was one of the best times of my life — I was young and life was great. I stayed there for seven months and it was long enough to learn a lot about myself.

In 1959, I entered the military academy. I had passed all the examinations and even got five extra points so I did not even need to be called before the credentials committee. Back then, the credentials committee was like a board of people that would interview you and decide whether you would be accepted or not. But it was not necessary for me to attend it — I was accepted based on my great results.

I remember I had money for a ticket to Kiev and one *pirojok* and I needed to get to Belaya Tserkov to see my wife. I was so

---

[5] Khrushchev's Virgin Lands campaign began in 1954 and was designed to open up parts of the steppe in the Kazakh SSR and the Altai region for cultivation. Settlers were sent to live there and farm the land. Soldiers, students, and others were sent there temporarily, to help them.

happy that I'd been accepted to school! I didn't even go back to the army barracks to pick up my things. I had submitted an application for three years in a row and hadn't got any reply. My documents had vanished without any reply. My platoon was performing well and my portrait hung on the wall of honor. I was the one and only captain of Jewish nationality. In the army, it is rude to distinguish by nationality. But, once, my commander told me: "You know why you haven't been accepted? Because you are a Jew."

When the commander of my regiment called me into his office, I told him that if I wasn't accepted into the academy the next year, I would leave the army. I don't know. It was possible to start drinking like many people did so they would get fired. So, he promised me that my documents would reach the academy. He promised to track my documents and I was accepted.

When I left to go and study, I told my wife that I would come back the following summer to Belaya Tserkov and we would get married. It didn't turn out that way because she was too young — she was in her last year in high school. But, in the winter, I got ill, began to miss her and kept looking at the picture I had of her. So I decided to go to Belaya Tserkov and get married in the winter. And we married on January 30, 1960.

Next year we will celebrate our fiftieth anniversary. Well, then we lived in an apartment in Penza for five and a half years. The apartment was very small and our son was born there in 1962. We were very poor and even collected firewood in the woods. Near us, in a dormitory, there were officers from the socialist block. However, we didn't have a room in this dormitory. But, later, in the sixth year, we got a room there and it was so much better than living in a basement apartment.

In 1965, I graduated. I had studied well, received a diploma with distinction, and they sent me to Dalniy Vostok [the Russian Far East], and sent others to Europe [a more desirable posting]. Even poor students were transferred to the Baltic states. I protested, but I was told that I would not be allowed to go. But I was sent to Novosibirsk instead of Dalniy Vostok and we stayed there for five years. There, I was promoted to the rank of major.

In 1970, I arrived [in Bishkek] as the military representative at a factory in Kyrgyzstan. I got 11 military awards, but it wasn't a big deal. After all, I hadn't participated in any wars.

I like music. I studied the accordion at a recreation center. I began to play, but when my sister died, I could not study anymore. I enjoyed photography for a while. Then I began to collect badges — I have a map of the Soviet Union made of badges from each city. I don't belong to any religion — I just believe in kindness. All the precepts dictated by religion are already in my heart. My wife, my son and I are always ready to help.

As for a hobby, I publish books devoted to military medals. When I retired, the factory was supposed to produce a medal. The man in charge of it was fired and the agreement to produce the medals had already been signed and could not be delayed. It turned out that I was nearby, so they asked me to produce the medals. Since I was a good technologist, it was not difficult to make the medals. Plus, I was assisted by designers and other staff. I was the first in Kyrgyzstan to produce these medals. You can find out more about it in my book.

8. The Principal

Gafurjon Shakirov, who is Tajik, was born in 1953 in Uchkurgan, a village in the Batken province of Kyrgyzstan, not far from Tajikistan. After graduating from university he became a teacher, and later, a school principal. "I am not a very religious person because I graduated from a university of Marxism-Leninism and my life has been devoted to that science. Still, I am a Muslim," he says. Nazarbegim Muzaffarova interviewed him in Uchkurgan on March 13, 2009.

In Uchkurgan, the collectivization policy was very strict. If anyone refused to collectivize, he was called a *kulak*. Earlier, there was a proletarian dictatorship, and it dictated to take away everything from *bays* [rich men] and distribute it to the people. There was no place for *bays* among ordinary people — *bays* were the minority.

World War II was the cruelest war that has ever happened in the world. In that war, 50 million people died. During the war, of course, life was very bad and there were many difficulties. Women worked from morning until night and there was a slogan: "everything for the front." We lost our two grandfathers during this war. It wasn't until five or six years after the war that quality of life began to rise again.

Hunger was a big problem during the war. In the Uchkurgan orphanage, children were so hungry that they ate grass and, as a result they died. If even two pieces of grain were stolen, the person who stole them might be arrested. In Uchkurgan, there was a military camp, which is why there were many Russians here and that had a big effect on the development of our village after the war. The effect of the Russians was very positive. We learned their culture and they learned ours. Many dance clubs and skating-rinks and other good things opened.

I was born into a family of *kokhozniki* [collective farmers].

We raised cotton. Since the end of the Soviet era, agriculture has changed. During the Soviet period, we raised cotton but, since 1990,[6] there is tobacco and now everyone who wants to grow anything is growing tobacco. Also, some agricultural professions have disappeared. There isn't an agronomist in our village now, or a veterinarian. And now there is a lack of equipment.

I went to school in my own village, at Secondary School No. 22. We studied in the Tajik language. I graduated in 1970. When I was in the first grade, we studied in an old school, which was like a mosque. Starting in the first grade, there was a lot of competition among students. Even our parents used to compete over whose child was more intelligent. It was very good. Unfortunately, now there is no longer such a tradition. We started to study at 9 a.m. and finished at 2 p.m. The teachers were well qualified and, even now, I can remember biology, I can solve mathematical and chemistry problems. My favorite subject was history.

Women have played a big role in my life, because I was raised by my mother — my father died when I was very young. My mom got up early in the morning, went to work and stayed there until the evening. Because of my mother — seeing that she was very worn out and it was hard for her to raise four children alone — we tried hard to study and graduate from school with honors. I know that my mother heroically played the role both of our mother and our father. These days, the number of men who are employed is very small and most men emigrate to Russia. They send money from there. Women are primarily responsible for raising the children.

The role of men here was very strong until the 60s and 70s. After 1970, the number of educated women was much higher than the number of educated men. During those years, after graduating from universities and getting jobs, women in Uchkurgan took on the same roles as men in families and in

---

[6] Kyrgyzstan became an independent state in 1991.

society. The role of children always was — and still is — the most important in every family. And you know, the more children there are in a family, the happier the family will be.

I got my higher education in Tajikistan. I graduated from the Tajik Pedagogical Institute in Leninabad. While I was there, I got a Kalinin Scholarship. Out of 15,000 students, only five of us got this scholarship.

I was also in the Komsomol and was a member of the municipal committee of the Komsomol. During university, I was very active in helping those who were not very good at studying. I helped them with philosophy, political economy, history of the KPSS [Communist Party of the Soviet Union] and scientific communism.

Those classes were very hard to understand and I tried to help them. During the Soviet era, to be uneducated was a big tragedy. There were situations when people who didn't pass their exams at universities committed suicide. To get a higher education was everyone's dream.

After graduation, the Ministry of Education sent me to my own village to work as a teacher at Secondary School No. 22. In 1976, I was sent to study at the Marxism-Leninism University of the Kyrgyz Communist Party. I graduated in 1980 and became a propagandist for the District Committee.

For 35 years, I worked in the pedagogical system. During my pedagogical career, I worked as an assistant principal and a principal, and — for three or four sessions — I was a deputy in the local *kenesh* [city council].

I am not a very religious person because I graduated from a university of Marxism-Leninism and my life has been devoted to that science. Still, I am a Muslim. During the Soviet era, the propaganda about atheism was very strong. At that time, we were taught to be godless. Still, there are more than a few religious people.

During Islamic holidays like Ramadan or Kurman Ait,[7] people always remembered their dead relatives. Kurman Ait was celebrated even during the Soviet times. The only difference was that the state did not celebrate the holiday and it was not a "red day" on the calendar, so people worked that day. No one had the right not to come to work on that day. If any worker — even a chief — didn't come to work, he was immediately called in by the district committee and discharged. But now [Kurman Ait] is a red day on the calendar and all the people of our republic have that day off. I don't read *namaz* [pray], but I know it. During the Soviet times, there were mosques, but they were only visited by pensioners. People under 60 years old were not allowed to visit mosques. Moreover, they didn't have time to go there — they were very busy with their work.

There is a ritual called *hijrat* Mecca. This is one of five things that a really religious person must do. *Hijrat* Mecca means making a pilgrimage to Mecca. Unfortunately, not all people are able to go there, because of financial limitations. But if a Muslim has an opportunity to visit that place, he must make the pilgrimage. Also, there is a ritual called *hanta*. If there is a son in the family, then this has to happen — it is a circumcision ritual. Such rituals bring people together.

I got married in a very ordinary way, just like all my friends. I became acquainted with my wife in a normal way. I had a friend, Abdurahman Sydykov. I often visited him in his house and it was there that I met her — she was his sister. We didn't communicate much, but we knew that we liked each other and she wanted to marry me, as at that time I was very solid — I was a sportsman — and was a cute guy and she was the niece of the first public prosecutor of the Tajik SSR. Now I have three children and one grandson.

---

[7] Also known as Eid al-Adha, Kurban Ait, or Kurban Bayram, it is a Muslim festival that commemorates the story of Ibrahim's willingness to sacrifice his son Ishmael as an act of obedience to God. For Christians, this is the story of Abraham and Isaac.

I love poetry, I like to read books, and sometimes I write poems. When I was young the most popular type of entertainment was sports. Television appeared in our community in 1959-1960, and there was only one channel that was shown. It was the Tashkent channel. Before television appeared, people often went to the cinema.

My first language is Tajik. I speak Uzbek, Russian, Afghan [sic] and Iranian. I learned all of those languages in my village. At school, I studied Russian and Uzbek. At home, we speak Tajik and, at work, I use Uzbek and Tajik. Of course, some languages are more prestigious than others. Nowadays, if a person wants to be well-educated, he has to know at least Russian or English. My favorite language, in which I prefer to speak all the time, is of course, Tajik. But with every representative of any nationality, I try to speak in the language of the nationality the person represents.

My favorite food is *plov*.[8] The way we make plov hasn't changed completely, but different recipes for making it have appeared. I eat a lot of food with meat. I know that it hurts [my health], but I eat it anyway. When a person becomes older, even eating habits change. For example, when I was young, I ate a huge amount of *plov* and fatty foods, but now I am afraid to eat it. The doctors do not allow me to eat it, because of my heart. Now, the word "cholesterol" has appeared in my vocabulary. When I was young, I never knew what that word meant.

---

[8] Lamb pilaf.

9. THE FAVORITE CHILD

Dilrom Ergasheva, who is Tajik, was born in 1951 in Uchkurgan, a village in the Batken province of Kyrgyzstan, not far from Tajikistan. She grew up on a collective farm, went to university, and became a teacher. "I never met [my husband] until the wedding. The first time I saw him was on the day of the wedding," she recalled. Nazarbegim Muzaffarova interviewed her in Uchkurgan on March 13, 2009.

I grew up in a very simple but educated family. I am the youngest child in my family: there were three girls and one boy. My father was in World War II — he went all the way to Berlin. During the war, my cousin and my grandfather died. The food situation was very difficult and my mother always told me that the women did men's work. They plastered, hauled stones, and built walls. Then, since my mother had three children, she was given easier work, drying products like potatoes and beets and sending them to the front.

My eldest sister helped my mother while my father was at the front. My other sister was born during the war, in 1943, and it was hard for my mother to do everything herself. My eldest sister used to wake up at 2 a.m. and go to stand in line to get bread; there were some cruel women who pushed her out of the line sometimes. Some immigrants— Poles and Chechens — were brought to our village and they were put in different houses. A Polish family lived in our house.

When my father came home, he worked on the collective farm, growing wheat. Our farm was divided into three parts, but there was only one chairman: Masadyrov. My father was a supply manager. We also grew tobacco and cotton. Earlier, during the Soviet times, agriculture was much better than it is now, because we worked collectively and everyone was provided with equipment. After the Soviet Union collapsed, all the land was divided up and sold. There was equipment of all sorts, there was fertilizer. After the collapse, everything changed.

Under collectivization, even though people were not educated, they worked hard and with great pleasure. My mother told me they used to take their children 3-4 kilometers from their homes, since that's where the farm was. They would put them in a wheelbarrow and take them to work. They never left their children with their mothers-in-law back then. On the farm, they had a nanny and she looked after their babies while they picked cotton.

Under collectivization, people were more interested in their work and there was unity and women had time to work on the farm and at home. We cannot say that one period of life was bad and another was good — people can get used to anything. During the Soviet era, there weren't any problems — the government helped with everything — but now everyone lives in their own way and nobody cares about others.

When we were young, the most popular kinds of entertainment were sports and dances. I, myself, was very good at sports — I was a basketball player. Our community first got television in 1954-55. Before that, people just worked. My mother and my grandmother sewed different kind of things: *tubetey*s — the Uzbek national head-dress; special dresses for brides; specially designed belts for men — for old people there was one kind of design, for young people there was other kind of design and the colors of the belts and their designs were important.

My mother was a seamstress and when she went to work, she took me to kindergarten. I remember my teacher, Tamara Nikiforovna, had perfect psychological approach to dealing with children. I loved her very much. I even called her my "second mother." When my own mother cursed me, I would tell her I wouldn't come home from kindergarten — I would stay with my second mother.

After I finished kindergarten, I went to the A. S. Pushkin

School — it was a Russian-language school. My father always brought me to school in his car, since I was the favorite child in the family. During the Soviet era, it was very good to be a student. There were many Russian teachers. My teacher was Valentina Sergeevna Semenova. Her son, Vitya, was my classmate. I hated mathematics; I loved history. I remember Roza Sungatovna, the math teacher, always told me that I had an empty head and understood nothing about math. On the evening of our graduation, she even went to my father and told him: "Your daughter is a good student, but please, do not send her to a university where she will have to study math — she doesn't understand math."

I graduated from school in 1969. Then I went to Fergana and entered the Department of Foreign Languages at the university there. I studied English. After graduation, I was assigned to work as an English teacher in my own region, in the Sukhana secondary school in Kyzylkiya.

In my family we spoke Tajik and Russian, but I couldn't speak literary Tajik. Even within our village there are many dialects of Tajik. When I worked as a teacher in the Sukhana school, there were Kyrgyz students and it was very hard for me to teach them because I didn't speak Kyrgyz at all, but the assignments in the books were in Kyrgyz.

I remember my first class with Kyrgyz students. They were eleventh graders. I introduced myself and said: "Guys, I don't know Kyrgyz so I will teach you English and you will teach me Kyrgyz." I would write the assignment on the blackboard and when the students did the work, I asked how it would be translated into Kyrgyz and they translated it for me and that was the way I learned Kyrgyz. I worked there for three years and, in that time, I learned Kyrgyz.

After three years of working there, I transferred to my own village — Uchkurgan. The situation was similar: here there were Tajik students and, with their help, I learned literary Tajik.

For every person, his own language should come first, and, after that, our state languages: Kyrgyz and Russian. Without knowing Russian, it is very hard to go to university. A knowledge of languages opens doors to friendship and unity. Now people are more developed in the language sphere; now they are more civilized. I remember when we were in school, the mountain kids never came down from the mountains. It was the older people who came down, and they just visited our bazaars, bought what they needed, and went back. But now their young people are studying in universities, getting educated and speaking different languages perfectly.

In Uchkurgan, I married and started a family. My husband was Sydyk Yakubov. We were born in the same year, but he was six months older than me. I never met him until the wedding. The first time I saw him was on the day of the wedding. He also studied in Fergana, at the polytechnic institute. I studied in a Russian school as a child and so, when I got married, people called me *Orus kelin* [Russian bride].

When I was young, I was a very fashionable woman. I liked to wear beautiful clothes. Also I liked talking with my relatives and I had many relatives who were living in Uzbekistan and we were always going there. We were very hospitable people. My mother was always saying that she had three tablecloths and that she knew how to welcome every kind of guest. If the guest is European, she welcomes him in European style; if he is Muslim, she welcomes him according to Muslim norms; if the guest is Asian, she welcomes him in Asian style. And she always said: "Look, the perspective of every nation is different, that is why you have to adjust."

During the Soviet era, no one from our family went to the mosque, but they knew about their religion. After the Soviet Union collapsed, strange people came here and forced women to wear the *hijab*. I didn't like it at all. Everyone should worship God however he wants. We believe in Islam, but I do not allow my children to go to mosques.

There were moments when parents of some of the children I was teaching came and asked me to dismiss their children from classes because they needed to go to mosque every Friday. But we were not allowed by our management to let the children to go. We taught the children to be atheists; I was always telling my students what is good and what is bad and that, if they were going to a Soviet school, they had to obey its rules. Even in universities, our professors were always telling us that, even though they were teaching us to be godless, they themselves believed in God. Now I read *namaz* [pray]; when I was younger, I never thought that someday I would read *namaz*. During the Soviet era, there were mosques, but they were visited only by old people.

The role of women has changed over the years. Now women are at the same level as men. Women do different kinds of work and, at the same time, they have to look after their families. Now there are more women that are supporting their husbands, than husbands supporting their wives.

I have four children: two daughters and two sons. My eldest daughter was born in 1983. She studied economics at an institute in Bishkek. My older son, Masrur, was born in 1987 and studies at the same institute, but in the correspondence school. My daughter Tasanno was a student at the Mountain Technical College. This year she finished that school and was accepted to another school, in the bookkeeping program.

My youngest son will finish school this year. We lost our dad in 2000, and I support the family myself. I am not complaining, though. I am trying and everything I do is turning out okay.

10. The Ladies' Man

Mikhail Bibikov, who is Russian, was born in 1926 in the village of Petrovka in the Chui province of Kyrgyzstan. He worked on a collective farm until he was called up to serve in the army in 1944. "It was my first time under enemy fire. I don't remember how long the Germans bombed us, but it seemed like it lasted for an eternity," he recalled. After the war, he returned to Kyrgyzstan and worked on the railroad until he retired. Dinara Davlembaeva interviewed him in Petrovka on March 13, 2009.

Even when I was a child, I had to work to feed my family. I had no time or opportunity to finish more than four classes in a village school, because I had to support a brother, two sisters, and my mother. At an early age, I started to work on the *kolkhoz* [collective farm]. I pulled beets from the fields and put them into a truck. Later, I drove a truck in from the fields and distributed the beets to the appointed places. Every morning, I got up to sit at the steering wheel and ride through the dusty roads and fields in the rain and the heat. In the evening, I hurried home to help my mother and my sisters around the house.

It was not difficult; I did not even get tired. My youth gave me a lot of energy. At the age of 14, my life resembled the daily routine of an adult man. From spring to autumn, the whole family was involved in chores in the garden. In the spring we hoed the entire garden and then planted potatoes, cucumbers, tomatoes, peppers, and so on. And in late summer and autumn, we harvested it all to eat and to conserve in jars for the long winter. Finally, we had to weed the garden before the cold weather. There is twice as much work in the village as in the city.

Life was quiet, but not easy. I started to date a girl and even wanted to marry her, but it never happened. In 1944, I was called up to serve on the front. I was 18 years old. That day I came home, entered the house, and saw my mother sitting at the kitchen table. She didn't say anything. I saw the call-up paper and understood everything without words. I remember the tears of my mother and sisters. My heart felt like it was going to break when I saw the looks in their eyes. My elder brother had been sent to the front before me. I promised to come back. Later that day I met my girlfriend and asked her: "Will you wait for me?" and she answered: "Yes."

Initially, I was sent to a Tashkent college with an artillery training regiment from the town of Chirchik [Uzbekistan]. Here, other young soldiers and I were trained to manage military equipment and to shoot serious weapons. I stayed in Uzbekistan for three months. I learned to shoot a 45 millimetre anti-tank gun. At the time, I did not understand the true face of war.

During training, they turned young and inexperienced men into well-trained soldiers. Later that same year, we went to Dnepropetrovsk [Ukraine], where we were to meet with commanders, colonels and generals. On the way to Dnepropetrovsk the train was stopped and all the passengers were asked to line up on the platform quickly. "Whoever can work with guns, three steps ahead!" a commander ordered. Three of my comrades and I stepped forward and the rest of the team got back in the train. We were taken to join Kharkov's 46th Tank Training Regiment.

In the town of Chiguev, near Kharkov [Russia], we were taught to drive tanks, shoot and live in dugouts in the forest. Our education did not take long. In the autumn of 1944, we finished our training and entered a military unit. As soon as possible, we began to load the tanks on the platform to be sent to the front. This moment was a turning point in my life. My comrades and I left for the long journey towards the destination called "war."

The road was painful. On the one hand, there was fear of the horrors of the war, fear for our lives, fear that we would never see our relatives, friends and loved ones again, would never embrace our mothers and would not kiss our girlfriends again. And I guess we all prayed that the road would never end. On the other hand, all these thoughts became so painful and endless that the soldiers started going mad and the longer they were on the road, the more they wanted to plunge into the action, to engage in battle with Nazis. At least, that's how I felt.

Eventually, after the long journey, a team of gunners and tankers, including me, went to the Belarusian Front, where there was fighting. That's when the war started for me. We arrived in the evening. That night, we just went to sleep.

Our first days on the Belarusian Front were quiet. There was no military activity so we tried to lead a normal life, enjoy conversation with our friends, play cards. In the evening, to keep our spirits up, to forget the harsh realities of our lives, we drank some alcohol. It warmed our hearts and, in the late autumn, it warmed our bodies, too. There were two more weeks left before the cold weather. For a while, we led relatively ordinary lives, but it didn't last long.

On the night of the second day of our stay in the camp, the fascists opened fire on the village and the house where all the soldiers were sleeping. Some fled for cover; others took up guns. The enemy had the advantage of surprise. It was my first time under enemy fire. I do not remember how long the Germans bombed us, but it seemed like it lasted for an eternity. I sat and covered my ears and looked around, lost, until Kolya shoved me.

Kolya was a friend of mine in the war. By the way, we met again after we were demobilized. Fortunately, we not only survived the war, but, on a fluke, had a couple of days at a resort together almost 20 years later. I went to Crimea to relax with my friends, using tickets I was given because I was a railway station worker. I didn't take my wife to the resort — it was a men's trip. There, we — old friends and colleagues — met each other on the street. Kolya did not recognize me at first. Twenty years had left their marks on my face; numerous wrinkles covered his face and my face. Kolya invited me into his apartment, where we spent all day reminiscing about the past, talking about the present, and sharing our plans for the future. We drank a lot that day.

Back to the war and the events of the second day of our stay on Belarusian Front: During the battle, one soldier got shot before he even managed to wake up. He died while he was sleeping. Perhaps he was dreaming about home, his family, and the blue sky.

All of us went crazy during the war. We reminisced about our relatives, our loved ones. It was so pleasant when we received the letters from home. The war frightened young guys so much that they resorted to various deceptions and tricks to be sent home. I remember the story of one of my countrymen, who, during an encounter with the fascists, deliberately shot himself inthe leg.He gave such a great performance to convince all of us that it was real that he was sent back home immediately and even given a medal for bravery.

Over time, I started to get used to the reality of war. It became easier to look at the dead. I had been in the war for about five months when, on a happy spring day, our victory over fascism was declared.

The war took away the lives of millions of people. Among them was my brother, Peter Bibikov, who died on the front as a result of an accident at the age of 21, in 1941. Peter's job was to transport shells on a cart. As a result of some strange circumstances, the cart overturned and a heavy metal shell fell on Peter and killed him. One of our countrymen who was there told my family the details of the fatal occasion. Such a stupid accident.

I did not return home immediately after the war. For another six years, I was far away from home. Almost all the soldiers who were with me in the 46th Tank Training Regiment stayed in Belarus for several years to train other young soldiers to shoot, drive tanks, and use the different weapons we had used during the war. Finally, in 1951, I was demobilized.

I did not think about where to go to live after demobilization. My homeland and my relatives were waiting for me. My mother and my sisters had expected me much earlier, and my girlfriend hadn't been able to wait. I asked her to wait for me, but when I returned I found out that she had gotten married. She hadn't even sent me a letter.

I needed a job, so I started thinking about possible sources of income. In 1951, I started working as a senior conductor at Pishpek [Bishkek] station. I had to accompany various goods to the town of Rybachie [Balykchy], which is in Issyk-Kul *oblast* [province], and back. I worked in this position until 1953. I did not like living in Pishpek and always being on the move. I wanted to return to Petrovka.

I remember in detail all the affairs I had before my marriage. For example, working in the city, I had a relationship with a girl. But I spent the majority of my time at work and she always complained I didn't give her enough attention.

I got tired of the city. Neither ladies nor my personal life brought me satisfaction. So, in 1953, I got transferred to work as a switchman on the railway in my native village. Working as a switchman, I controlled the railways. These days trains have become an unpopular mode of transport, but many years ago, when there were no cars and planes were rare and expensive pleasures, work on the railways was in full swing. My duty was to switch the rails, to determine the route of the oncoming train.

Life in Petrovka was much more fun for me. There, I got the reputation of a womanizer. A lot of girls liked me. I remember some of my romantic adventures very well. I had an educated girlfriend but I was not equal to her, because I hadn't finished school, not to mention university.

So, we couldn't be together, because of our unequal social statuses. The second girl, I left myself. She was an agronomist from the neighbouring village. I wanted to marry her, but changed my mind as soon as I found out that she decided to *prevorozhit* [bewitch] me.

I remember another case in detail. Once, in the evening, I went to see a girl. I remember the evening. We stood in a small wood between thin birches, under a bright moon. I stood close to her. I saw the shadow of two birch trees and our silhouette. And, hiding behind another tree, I saw the girl's mother. I didn't pay any attention. The time to say goodbye arrived and I started home. From afar I heard how the girl's mother order her not to date me. I became upset, and made up my mind not to approach her any more.

While I was single for a year and enjoying the bachelor's life, I met my current wife, Anna Timofeyevna. In 1954, a family from Siberia moved to the village of Belovodsk. I heard there was a young Siberian girl with the family. She impressed me from the first moment I saw her. She was different from the other women in the village. I liked her so much that I walked seven kilometres to see her every day, brought her flowers, and invited her to the cinema or to just walk. After some time, my family went to ask for her in marriage.

We didn't get married after the engagement. We just started to live together. Only a year and a half later, my wife and I had to register our relationship with stamps in our passports. The phrase "had to" is ideally suited to this situation, because neither she nor I thought about such conventions. We had decided to go on a holiday that was for married couples. So, we quickly arranged our marriage and went on our "honeymoon."

She was a little plump and very religious. I am not a religious man. I believe in God and that people are responsible for every good or bad deed. However, due to Anna, my family celebrates all the sacred holidays and fasts regularly.

Around this time, I was promoted to senior switchman at the same station. I worked in this position from 1955 to 1968. Then I was transferred into the other job, where my colleagues and I had to inspect 10 kilometres of rail every day. This work was very important because bad rails and ties could cause accidents and threaten the lives of passengers.

In addition to my work on the railroad, I was chairman of the local committee and the committee on protection of labour and wages for 32 years. My responsibilities included the organization of weekly meetings to discuss financial incentives for hard workers and to control over-charging. I checked whether citizens' work was evaluated correctly. At that time, the principle of "thirteenth [monthly] salary" was very popular. It was issued to successful and hard-working employees.

In 1983, I resigned due to illness. But my restless nature didn't allow me to sit at home and just farm. I didn't want to lie on the couch as long as my physical strength and health allowed me to work. So I started working in the kindergarten of the collective farm as a clerk.

Now I am an old father of four children — two sons and two daughters — a grandfather, and even a great-grandfather. I gave all of my children higher education. My eldest daughter, Nina, who now lives in the village, graduated from the Samarkand Institute of Economics. My son, Kolya, born in 1958, finished vocational school, became an electrician, and now lives in Germany. My younger daughter, Tatyana, got an economics degree and now lives in Russia. My youngest son, Mikhail, who was named after me, lives with me and my wife and helps us around the house. His wife helps Anna with milking the cow, cooking, and other things.

I like my life. I wouldn't change anything, even if I was given the opportunity to change my fate. Despite a small pension of 3,000 *som*s [about $71], I even manage to help my children. Our own chicken, milk, and garden vegetables feed my family and my son's family. But I confess that it would not be bad if my pension were increased. Luckily, I get veteran's benefits and financial support from the railroad. The previous year, I received 40,000 *som*s from them.

11. THE PARTY SECRETARY

Kurman-Ghali Karakeev, who is Kyrgyz, was born in 1913 in the village of Kermenty in Issyk-Kul province, Kyrgyzstan. Though he expected to grow up to be a farmer or shepherd, he rose instead to become the secretary of the Central Committee of the Communist Party of the Kyrgyz Soviet Socialist Republic (SSR) and, later, the president of the Academy of Sciences of the Kyrgyz SSR. Dinara Davlembaeva interviewed him in Bishkek on March 18, 2009.

I was born into a poor, rural family near the coast of Lake Issyk-Kul. It was so many years ago, we still used the old calendar.[9] Like the rest of the rural population, I could pasture sheep and breed livestock and I never thought about education or science. But my destination was not what I expected and my parents made a great contribution to it. My fate started becoming apparent even at an early age. I was a distinctive child, a bright leader, with a creative streak.

My parents sent me to school. Few parents were concerned about the education of their children in the village in those years. After school, I entered Issyk-Kul Agricultural College. During college, I started to get involved in Party activities. At the age of 16, I joined the Komsomol.

Not surprisingly, the Party soon invited me to work as a journalist for the national youth newspaper Leninchil Zhash. From that time onward, I moved up the career ladder quickly. First, I became a chief of department, and later the editor of the newspaper — a great success for a young boy. From 1934 to 1936, I worked as a head of the department of students at the Kyrgyz Regional Committee VLKSM.[10]

---

[9] Until the revolution in 1917, Russia still used the Julian calendar, rather then the Gregorian.

[10] *Vsesoyuzni leninskii kommunistichiskii soyuz molodyozhi* [All-Union Leninist Young Communist League], better known as the Komsomol.

Then the war years came and I was called up to serve in the in the Black Sea navy. Actually, I was very happy for the chance to serve at sea, because I was born near Lake Issyk-Kul and I felt right at home on the water. There, I completed my political training with honours and actively participated in the life and work of the military unit. For my accomplishments, the leadership of the navy personally wrote a thank-you letter to my parents.

It was not easy to work in leadership positions during World War II. But I was a member of the Communist Party, I became deputy editor of the magazine Communist, and at the same time held the position of secretary of the Tian-Shan and Issyk-Kul party committees. My responsibility was organizational work. I was so touched by the troubles of the people and the fate of the country that my heart was bleeding all the time. I worked 24 hours a day, without sleep. I thought out and organized charitable actions to ease the heavy burdens of the soldiers in the war. For example, during one charity event, I gathered a considerable amount of clothing and food and personally accompanied it into blockaded Leningrad.

The pain of millions of people, their spiritual wounds, the tears they shed for all the human losses, the hundreds of destroyed cities and villages, pushed me to document these historical events. I have written about the Stalinist repression of 1937-1938, and the Great Patriotic War [World War II]. I knew all the different perspectives on these events, since at that time, on the one hand, I represented the members of the party — the elite — and on the other hand, I was a representative of the ordinary population, raised in a poor village family.

From 1944 to 1946, I was a student in the Party School of the CPSU [Communist Party of the Soviet Union] Central Committee in Moscow. And then I became an editor of the national newspaper Sovetik Kyrgyzstan and, later, the secretary of the Central Committee of the Communist Party of Kyrgyzstan.

A part of my political life was my work as a propagandist. During the post-war period, it was necessary to raise the patriotic spirit of the people. From 1946 to 1956 I was involved in campaigning for morality, patriotism, friendship among nations, and internationalism. I always did everything selflessly. It's part of my character. I was a real patriot. I considered it my personal duty to work for the sake of the motherland.

After graduating from the Higher Party School, I entered into a system where special staff were prepared to educate young people. The main tasks at that time were the improvement of operational management and the promotion of the economy and culture of the country. A series of reforms concerning the forms and methods of political education in the Komsomol were implemented to achieve those goals. By the way, I published some books containing my personal works and experiences during that time.

In February of 1946, I was involved in social and political campaigns leading up to the elections for the Supreme Soviet of the USSR. We organized campaign groups. We trained campaign teams to inform people about the elections. We prepared lectures and reports on the principles of Soviet democracy, the electoral system, and the Constitution. I have published a book about the organization of the Soviet political system, based on my personal experience and knowledge.

The task of the party was to develop the national economy. Cultural educational institutions were strongly involved in propaganda activity. Great importance was attached to lectures about social and political themes. To increase awareness among the people, I was involved in economic education.

Literature didn't escape the Party's attention, either. The Party emphasized art as a way of promoting ideology. The goal was to develop all genres of fiction. But, by the 90s this niche was filled by Western fiction. National folk art and amateur art was crowded out.

I was involved in cultural, social, economic, and political reorganizations. I was part of the system that created history, created the state's structure, and promoted ideology. At different times I felt the joy of victory, the bitterness of defeat, and, eventually, the destruction of our ideals. A republic with cultural and intellectual potential broke up before my eyes. It was difficult to see how the world the Party had built was being ruined.

A member of the Central Committee of the Communist Party of Kyrgyzstan, a delegate to the twenty-second, twenty-third, and twenty-fifth conventions of the CPSU, a deputy of the Supreme Soviet of the USSR, and the Supreme Soviet of the Kyrgyz SSR — these were my public activities. Anyone interested in politics would be jealous of these successes. But, after all this political activity, I changed my perspective on my work. I wanted to do something else.

After earning my Ph.D. at the CPSU Central Committee's Academy of Social Sciences in 1959, I was appointed president of the Academy of Sciences of the Kyrgyz SSR. During my two decades of service there, the Academy achieved enormous things. And they were not only for the scientific community, but for the country as a whole.

In 1954, the National Academy of Sciences (NAS) of the Kyrgyz SSR was founded as a branch of the USSR Academy of Sciences. It gathered together the most prominent and distinctive personalities of the time. It involved about 1,200 workers, 550 of whom were doctors and or "candidates" of the sciences.

The NAS cultivated new professionals and contributed to an increase in Kyrgyzstan's scientific potential. The results of our years of work were the development of major theoretical propositions and valuable practical advice; and an increase in the efficiency of scientific and technological progress. This, in turn, promoted economic development, exploitation of natural resources, increased productivity, and improved production technology.

I will name a few of the achievements of the specialists of the Academy during the period when I headed it: Kyrgyz scientists created a geological map predicting where rare minerals could be found, carried out space research, and developed machinery for collecting soil samples on the Moon. Also, it was during this time that Academician P.I. Chalov made his discovery about uranium. Over the years, the Academy of Sciences has made contributions to the development of the Kyrgyz language. It has also studied folk art, literature, and the Manas epos.[11] In 1965, a Kyrgyz-Russian dictionary was published. The Scientific Institute of Language and Literature under the Academy of Sciences was closely involved in working to improve the grammar of the Kyrgyz language by creating educational materials.

I am the author of more than 300 works, including monographs, books and pamphlets about history, beginning from the time of the Kara-Kyrgyz Autonomous Region[12] until the time of the creation of an independent Kyrgyzstan. Some of my works are: *The History of Cultural Construction in the Kyrgyz Republic*, and *The Great October Revolution and Science in Soviet Kyrgyzstan*.

Also, I supported the creation of such books as *The History of Communist Organizations in Central Asia, Omitting Capitalism on the Way to Socialism, The Participation of the Workers of the*

---

[11] An epic Kyrgyz poem, with nearly half a million lines. Manas is the hero's name.

[12] The area that is now known as the Kyrgyz Republic has gone through several name changes over the past century or so. When the Russians first arrived in the region, the Kyrgyz people were living under the Kokand *khanate*. After the *khanate* was destroyed in 1876 and the Kyrgyz submitted to Russian rule, they were absorbed into the Semirechie Oblast of Turkestan. In 1918, they were included in the new Turkestan Autonomous Soviet Socialist Republic, within the Russian Federation. In 1924, the area became the Kara-Kyrgyz Autonomous Oblast. In 1936, it became the Kyrgyz Soviet Socialist Republic, one of the Soviet Union's 15 republics. At that time, it was also known as Kirghizia. Now it is Kyrgyzstan or the Kyrgyz Republic.

Kyrgyz Republic in Building Socialism, *Celebration of the Ideas of the Great October Revolution*, *The All-Conquering Power of Leninist Ideas*, and *Problems in the Management and Construction of a Multinational Soviet State*.

Back then, the Academy of Sciences was effective. But the golden age of science in Kyrgyzstan was mainly during the Soviet era. Now, a lack of financing, combined with higher prices for equipment, materials, services, and so on, are making trouble for science in Kyrgyzstan. Over time, research is becoming more difficult. I am disappointed that the development of science here has almost stopped. For many years, the Academy has not been receiving enough attention, but despite this, its staff continue to work for the present and the future of Kyrgyzstan.

Even after I left the presidency of the Academy, I continued to help students and monitor the results of their work. I was asked for advice and I did not decline to help young scientists, because doing so is not work, but pleasure. Students of promise, some of whom later became professors at universities and headed scientific institutions, came out from under my wings. I supervised and assisted with 20 master's and doctoral theses.

By now, the college where I studied in my youth is named in my honour. For all my achievements and contributions to science, the former President of the Kyrgyz Republic awarded me the Order of Manas. My name is mentioned in the *Great Soviet Encyclopaedia*, the *Historical Encyclopaedia*, the *Encyclopaedic Dictionary*, and the *History of Kyrgyzstan*.

12. The Miner

Abidjan Yuldashov, who is Uzbek, was born in 1935 in Osh, Kyrgyzstan. He went to work in a mine at the age of 14 and worked there as a miner and driver until he lost his sight at 50. "I wouldn't wish blindness on anyone," he said. Rayhon Jonbekova interviewed him in Navoi Park in Osh on March 10, 2009.

My parents are Uzbeks from the city of Osh. They were *bays* — rich people. My father was a blacksmith and he owned a lot of land. My parents willingly gave their land and horses to the government and left their fingerprints on the documents as their signatures. I still have those documents at home, but they are not necessary anymore.

I was born in 1935, but I got my passport two years later. So, in my passport, I was born in 1937. In my early childhood, we moved a lot. We didn't have anything. For lack of resources, during the war, we had to sell our house. Then we moved to Toshkumir and later came back to Osh again. My mother was alone. I was the smallest child in the family. My older brother was taken to the war and there was no one to take care of us.

There was no opportunity for me to go to school. After finishing the fourth grade, I went to work in the mine. Later, I went to evening school in Osh. It was an accelerated education. I finished seven grades, just by attending evening school. I didn't have shoes or many clothes. At school, we were sitting hungry and cold. We wanted to eat, but the instructor was asking us to learn and repeat. After the war, life continued to be difficult.

In Toshkumir I had to go to work in the mine when I was 14. At that time, no one asked for documents and I didn't have themanyway. After working for two years, I was asked to bring my documents. I received a salary, so I could get my passport and the other documents I needed. The work in the mine was hard. Not just men and children, but even women worked there. It was a harsh time. Mining is not an easy job.

Child labor was acceptable those days. In the mine, I worked with older guys. Back then, people were sensitive and cared about each other. I got the same salary as others, but they always pitied me and gave me easy work. "Bring us water," they would tell me.

I worked with Russians, Chechens, Tatars, Kyrgyz, and international people. We never paid attention to nationality. We were all equal and friendly. In the mine, I learned many languages. The number of Kyrgyz and Uzbeks was low in the mine. Mainly Russians and Tatars worked there. So I speak Tatar very well. When I speak Tatar, no one believes that I am Uzbek.

Once, while working in the mine, I was trapped in a collapse and hospitalized in Osh. After my treatment, I felt better and went back to work. I said that I was not injured anymore and got my job back. I worked as an excavator driver until I lost my sight. When I first became a driver, after working the mine, I thought that driving was also a hard job, but then it turned out to be easy.

I was about 50 years old when I lost my sight. After becoming blind, I never worked again. I lost my sight probably because of all the work I did when I was a child. It has already been 24 years. I lost it quickly. It happened like this: I was driving and another vehicle was coming the other way. He stopped, but I continued to drive and I hit him. He brought me water and asked whether I was drunk. But I never drink. I told him that, for some reason, I couldn't see — and he didn't believe me. Later, I got two operations on my eyes but it didn't bring back my sight.

Without my eyesight, it is difficult to wash myself and do other things. When a person is lame, it still easy, but without eyesight, it is terrible. I would not even wish this on my enemy. I cannot see light. I cannot determine what is beautiful and what is not. When my wife gives me something to eat, I can't see what it looks like. I wouldn't wish blindness on anyone.

Being young is very good, but when one becomes older, he is not needed that much. When a person is blind, it seems that he is a burden. The best years in life are from 18 to 55. In this period, one is very energetic. Later, one becomes tired easily.

I worked a lot in life, because I had many children. My first wife died 15 years ago. She got ill and died. She gave birth to 15 children. Three of them died in early childhood. She didn't work because she had lots of work to do at home. She always had to feed our children, cook, wash, and clean. Women's work is endless — it is hard even with just one child. Some men don't value women's work around the house, but they would never be able to do it themselves. When my wife died, four of my children were still small. I taught them everything.

For about six years, I have been living with another woman. She is 40 years younger than me, but she is ill. I help her by calming her down and she helps me with everything from cooking to washing. I give her her medicines on time. I think a family is happy and healthy when a wife and a husband support each other. [My second wife] is an orphan. She had a difficult life. She was often beaten by her first husband. She has one child. Sometimes I send her child to visit my daughters — otherwise he would be bored being with us all the time.

It is hard these days to find a job here. Everything is expensive. There is a lack of iron and construction materials. During the Soviet period, we had everything. Everything was available and sufficient. People say we fed Russia. It is Russia who fed and saved us. People didn't understand how Russia helped us to develop. Now we have become independent and nothing is available for ordinary citizens.

Before, when I became an invalid, everything was available for me. I would go to the government offices and they would listen to me, ask what I needed, and help me. We were given three tons of coal and wood. Nowadays, nothing is available for invalids and pensioners.

During, the Khrushchev era, life was difficult. He probably wanted to build democracy, but people didn't understand at first. When they understood, they got rid of him. During the Brezhnev era, life was good. Everything was cheap, starting with sausages, etc. Now, only rich people eat sausage. I, for example, near the bazaar, smell it and pass by, because I don't have money. Before, I could buy 14 sacks of flour on my salary.

From one perspective, things are good now: the people have gotten their independence. They can pray if they want to, and they can do whatever they want. It is good. The rich can buy cars and they can even own planes. In our times, everything was checked by the government: "Did he really earn that money or not?"

I have 12 children. My children, thanks to God, do not use drugs or alcohol, and they are not thieves. My children do not live here, but I am not mad at them, because, there are no jobs in Kyrgyzstan right now, so they had to leave. My daughters are living in Uzbekistan with their husbands. Just one is living in Kyrgyzstan. But my children come visit on holidays. My children help me, which is good because it would be hard to live by relying on my pension. My oldest daughter is 49. I have grandchildren and great-grandchildren. I visit them sometimes.

But, although they care for me in my old age, I like living here in my apartment.

Nowadays, the government itself is poor. There are many rich people, of course, but for the invalids and pensioners like me, life is very difficult. Still, we are surviving. The main things in my life are that the sky is blue, the water is clean and the sun is shining, which is very good.

13. THE EXILE

Akram Valiev, who is Bashkir, was born in 1913 in Bashkiria, Russia. He moved to Central Asia to escape arrest and became a teacher. "There was always bribery in the education system. I think it will never stop," he said. Rayhon Jonbekova interviewed him in Osh on March 11, 2009.

I was born in 1913 in a small village in Bashkiria [now Bashkortostan, in Russia]. My father was a *mullah* and a leader at the mosque. We were poor. When the revolution started in the 1920s [sic], my father was arrested for teaching religion. After that, he advised me never to go against the government and to be a productive member of society. He also told me that, if I wanted to study, I should go to Turkestan.

The people of Turkestan are a "golden" nation. In Turkestan, Bukhara is very well known for being a center of knowledge. In 1929, when I knew that I was on a list of those to be arrested, I took my father's advice and went to study. At the beginning, a Russian man took me to work with him. I worked on the railway. He was a kind man and got me Communist Party card. After a year, he advised me to study. In 1930, I studied for a year.

After finishing, I worked for a year as an instructor for young workers, to improve the literacy rate. At the end of the day one day, a Tatar Communist visited me and invited me to study with him. We both went to study in the city of Tomsk. From 1931 to 1933, I studied in Tomsk and worked there in a library, distributing newspapers. After that, I went to Bukhara to continue my education. There, I attended Rabfak [the workers' department]. The director of the Rabfak was an honest and fascinating Communist. In Rabfak, I studied on a full governmental scholarship. We got clothes, food, books — everything we needed to study. The only criterion for admission was knowledge of the Uzbek language.

Once there was an issue: Two students — a Russian and a Tatar — ran away from the institute. The head of the institute asked me to bring them back. "If they refuse, here is a package to give to the public security officer. Ask him to help," he told me. In the package there was a note, which said that the two students had stolen musical instruments. I found out that the father of the Tatar student was an attorney, so I brought them back without major difficulty. After this, I understood that the leader of Uzbekistan, Akmal Ikramov,[13] had a strict policy of educating all the native Uzbek speakers.

I finished Rabfak in 1937. In the same year, I attended the Gospedinistut [Government Pedagogical Institute] in Samarkand, majoring in physics and mathematics. I received a diploma, although I was a poor student. In Samarkand, I studied with the former Tajik Minister of Science, who was rich. When we went to parties, he gave me his suits to wear. He was a kind person.

After finishing my studies, I was sent to the army, to the 221st Company of sharpshooters. I was stationed in Russia, not far from Stalingrad. When the Germans attacked Stalingrad, we surrounded them. I was wounded in the war. I spent about

---

[13] First Secretary of the Communist Party of Uzbekistan from 1929-1937.

eight months in a hospital and was released from the army as an invalid. In 1943, I came to Osh. Life during the war was difficult. There were many hooligans in Osh then.

About that time, a university opened in Osh. I was a faculty member there for 17 years. In 1939, a teachers' institute opened and that's where I worked. Based on this institute, a pedagogical institute was later opened. I worked there as well. Based on the pedagogical institute, Osh State University was opened. I worked there until 1973. After that, I retired.

After becoming a pensioner, I started to write books. I taught mathematics and wrote books about it. Aside from mathematics, I wrote about spiritual education. I knew Arabic very well. I have many Muslim and Tatar calendars, which I translated. My books are available in some schools in Kyrgyzstan and in Bashkiria as well.

I wrote a book about the schools in Osh. From 1838 to 1875, five *madrassa*s were built. Over the next 19 years, eight schools were built here to teach the Koran. The first [non-Muslim] school was constructed by General Funkov. After the area became a part of Russia [of the Russian Empire], education became an important part of the culture.

When the first Russian language schools were opened in Osh, it was difficult for students to study in Russian. Many didn't go to school, but continued working until the revolution. In 1919, the Russian school was turned into a Kyrgyz-Uzbek school. In the 1950s, there was a project to open one local-language school for every 50 square kilometers. About 30 schools were opened in the Fergana Valley. The positive effect of the Russians coming here is that they opened many schools in Osh.

Once, an Uzbek student was late to school and the teacher beat him with a stick. The student went to his father, showed him his back, and told him that he didn't want to go to school anymore. Later, when the indigenous schools opened again, he went back to continue his studies and became an academic.

There was always bribery in the education system. I think it will never stop. One day, when I was teaching, a student came to me and offered me money. He asked me to help him with the graduation examination. I told him to take his money back and helped him for free. I didn't take bribes from students. But sometimes, when part-time students came down from the mountains, they brought *kumys*, *airan*, and *kaimak*[14] with them and gave it to me because, according to Muslim law, a student must thank his instructor. My father was a *mullah* and he taught *namaz* and Koran. He got presents, too. But I never forced my students to bring me anything.

In Kyrgyzstan, there was a lack of teaching resources. It was difficult for me to get started. I had to take Russian-language materials and translate them into Kyrgyz. I know all the Muslim languages: Kazakh, Uzbek, Bashkir, Tatar, and Arabic.

I am Bashkir and my wife was Tatar. She lived in Osh, but we met each other in Samarkand, where we studied together. She was a good student and a good instructor. We wrote to each other and then, in 1943, I came to Osh. We had two children. We lived together and, 10 years ago, she died. I didn't marry again, because I wanted to save the good memories that I had with my wife. A new wife could bring a new life and it might destroy some good memories from the past.

After it became a part of Russia, many Tatar people came to Kyrgyzstan. They taught religion here and had positive opinions about Kyrgyzstan. One of my friends, Musa Shavkat, had to leave Kyrgyzstan after 13 years. He wrote that he counted "the 13 years of [his] life in Osh as a life in Paradise." Another person said that Kyrgyz people are "golden." They are very friendly. Before, Kyrgyz people lived in the mountains, in *yurt*s. That was their life. Osh was mainly populated by

---

[14] *Kumys* is a dairy beverage made from slightly fermented mare's milk; *kaimak* is thick, homemade sour cream.

Bashkirs and Uzbeks. The people living in the cities were mainly educated people. The Kyrgyz people didn't know how much wealth they had. They didn't know how many cows or sheep they had. Before there were *bay*s [rich people], and *fakiri* [poor people]. After Kyrgyzstan became a part of Russia, Kyrgyz people's lives improved.

14. The Teacher

Abdukhapar Bekebaev, who is Kyrgyz, was born in 1945 in the village of Kyzl Suu, near Osh, Kyrgyzstan. He is a teacher. Rayhon Jonbekova interviewed him in Osh on March 11, 2009.

I was born into a well-educated family. There were 12 children in my family. My father was the chairman of a collective farm and we lived a good life. We had land, so we had enough food to eat and clothes to wear. My brothers and sisters all got higher educations.

After finishing high school, I studied at OGPI.[15] When I finished, there was only one university: Osh State University. After finishing, I stayed and taught there, like a good alumnus. I worked as a teacher all my life. I am still teaching at the same institute, in the General Education Department.

Before, the education system worked very well. The Soviet Union gave us a broad education. We studied a broad range of courses. Currently, of course there are many positive developments. For example, the specializations are narrower and more focused. Students take all the courses for their specialization and they also have the opportunity to choose classes by themselves. In our time, we were told which classes to take.

There is a big difference between the current generation and our generation. The older professors claim that students these days read less. I think students now live in different conditions. They use the Internet and, through the 'net can find all kinds of materials. They don't have to read several books in order to write a paper — it is easier to find summaries on the Internet. Once I told my student that he wrote avery good paper and said I thought he must have worked a lot on it. He told me that he found it on the Internet. It is technological

---
[15] *Oshski gumanitarnuyu-pedagogichiskom institutye* [Osh Humanities-Pedagogical Institute].

development. We didn't have such opportunities. The negative thing is that, nowadays, students don't read books. Russians read a lot, but Asians don't read much.

Osh is the oldest city in Kyrgyzstan. There is a second Osh, in France. Recently, we celebrated the 3,000th anniversary of Osh. The name "Osh" comes from a Chinese scientist, who spelled it "o-osh" (with two Os) meaning "to barter." The Silk Road ran through Osh and silk was brought from China and diamonds and other goods were brought from the West. So, Osh was a place where this barter between Chinese and Western merchants took place.

During the socialist regime, Kyrgyzstan was a place where animals were raised. There were also about 20 factories. But later, the leaders didn't pay enough attention to Osh, so it is not that developed.

Many holy monuments were destroyed. The politicians were against religion. For example: Babur's[16] house on Suleiman Mountain was destroyed.[17] And some *madrassa*s were destroyed; Alymbek Madrassa, for example, which was one of the biggest, was destroyed.

The Communists claimed religion was subversive. From one perspective, that was good, because a country will not be very well developed if it is too religious. For example: In Iran women wear the *hijab*. Does it mean that they are better than

---

[16] Babur (1483-1530), said to be a descendent of both Tamerlane and Chingis [Ghengis] Khan, was the founder of the Mughal Empire, which included part of present-day Afghanistan and much of present-day Pakistan and northern India. He was the son of the ruler of the Fergana Valley, which is now split between Uzbekistan and Kyrgyzstan (the city of Osh is located at its eastern end). His memoir, *The Baburnama*, is available in English.

[17] "Communist Party bosses had Babur's house torn down in the 1960s when the faithful from all over the region started coming there to worship and pray. The faithful rebuilt it again in the early 1990s," according to the July 27, 2007, article "Mount Suleiman Needs Protection," on the website *Ferghana.ru*.

we are? Does it mean that they are more developed? No. If religion was that helpful, they would live better than us. We have a balance between religion and economics.

Talking about political regimes, there have been two parts: the socialist regime, in the past; and the current, democratic regime. Both of these regimes have positive and negative sides. It is difficult to define democracy. Even Americans can't define the whole meaning of this word, although they have been living with it for about 200 years. In all democratic regimes, there should be strict rule of law. Without laws, a person is like a cockroach. In Kyrgyzstan, the leaders don't understand the word democracy. They lead in a more traditional way. But what they are doing is right, because, in our society, people do not understand freedom. Therefore, they jump too high, which is bad, because if they fall, it would be painful. Therefore they shouldn't jump that high.

Currently, people have more freedom than in the past. Kyrgyzstan, especially, is the most democratic country in Central Asia. In our republic, the political situation is stable, because we have a good group of politicians — the law should be strict.

America is a wise nation. We Asians, on the other hand, are trying to develop quickly, which is impossible. We need to go through the evolution of democratization. Right now, we are still very "young." We have to take steps, to learn and grow up.

15. The Alpinist

Alexander Eropunov, who is Russian, was born in 1929 in Kyzyl Asker, Kyrgyzstan. He is an alpinist. "I went on an expedition to Muztagh Ata, which is 7,450 meters tall, when I was 65 years old. I went there with Salamatin, my friend, and at the peak of the mountain, after three days, we celebrated our expedition by drinking vodka," he said. Maksat Annamuradov interviewed him in Bishkek on March 13, 2009.

I was born on May 1, a date which is now honored in Kyrgyzstan with mountain climbing competitions. The region that I was born in is now called Kyzyl Asker, but it used to be called Chyllou Kasak, Pishpek. My mother worked as a cleaner; she had studied in the high school for only three years. My father was chief of railway cargo control at Pishpek Station. His agency was responsible for hauling all types of cargo, since Pishpek [Bishkek], in those days, did not have any kind of mechanization.

My father died in 1941, during the battle for Moscow. He was an artillery soldier in the Panfilov Division, which included soldiers from Alma-Ata [Almaty] and Pishpek. His division saved the city of Moscow from the Nazis. The battle for Moscow was considered one of the cruelest of World War II. During that time I was a teenager and my family, which included three children, was experiencing its hardest days.

The war years were harsh. There was starvation, all the businesses were closed, and it was hard to find anything to eat. However, we had special cards that permitted us to get 100 grams of sugar per month and 200 grams of oatmeal per month. But no butter and no meat were available during those times. On the other hand, the atmosphere was very friendly. Everybody was supporting each other and sharing with each other, and there weren't different nationalities like Tatars, Kurds,

Azeris, etc. — there were just people, just citizens. In the those days, I was involved in gymnastics, diving, and wrestling.

Since I came from a poor family, my mother encouraged me to get an education. I graduated from the Pedagogical Institute in Pishpek in 1951. I was sent to the city of Osh to work as a teacher in the Physical Education Department at the Institute of Physical Culture. I later became the head of the department.

Despite the war, I saw German people as nice, hardworking people. We had Germans living here with us, in Chui province, in the city of Talas, and in other small towns of Kyrgyzstan. My relations with them were always good. I do not judge people by their nationalities. But, if I had a choice between Hitler and Stalin, I would choose Stalin, because he was continuing the politics of the great reformer, Lenin.

Even after the war, life did not get better. The conditions were harsh. However Stalin's death for me was not only the death of the chief of the Soviet Union, but also the loss of a leading figure, one that was important for the survival of our society.

Khrushchev, to me, was not a politician or a leader because he did not have an ideology. To me, he was just a specialist in agriculture, since as he previously had been involved in the agricultural development of the country. He was good for Ukraine, where he was the leader of the Central Committee of the Communist Party. He should have stayed there.

I became an alpinist and I loved climbing mountains. I received various awards and certificates of achievement for my alpinism. I became an alpinist because I performed well in a climbing competition that was held in Kyrgyzstan and people noticed me. One of my best awards was third place in the Soviet Union in high-altitude climbing, which I got when I climbed the Peak of Military Topographers, in the Tian Shan [in

Kyrgyzstan], which is 6,958 meters tall. I also received the rank of Master of Sports of the Soviet Union in alpinism. But the most beautiful peak that I have climbed was Kyzyl Agyn [in Kyrgyzstan], which is 6,950 meters tall.

I went on an expedition to Muztagh Ata [in China], which is 7,450[18] meters tall, when I was 65 years old. I went there with Salamatin, my friend, and at the peak of the mountain, after three days, we celebrated our expedition by drinking vodka. That is a tradition among alpinists. Also, my expedition to Peak Lenin,[19] which is 7,134 meters tall, was unique for me, since I organized it with a group of 70 people. I have one bad memory from my time as an alpinist: I almost died once; I was left under the snow and rescued later.

I am not an alpinist right now, but I am actively involved in the development of alpinism around the world. For instance, three months ago, I went to China to organize an expedition there. I was invited by a tour agency and the Chinese Embassy in Kyrgyzstan.

Through my mountain climbing, I have visited many countries: Austria, Czechoslovakia, China and others. Also, I was an assistant to the Minister of Sports and Culture of the Kyrgyz SSR from the 1960s until I became a pensioner. Also, I developed and built a school of boxing and wrestling in the 1970s.

I had very little time left after all of my work and my athletic life. But the time I did have, I spent with my wife, visiting theaters and cinemas — even in Moscow. I loved ballet. I watched all the performances back then. Here in Bishkek, I went to Beishenaliyeva's performances,[20] which were beautiful. In those times, however, the culture suffered from a lack of

---

[18] It is actually 7,546 meters tall.

[19] Now known as Ibn Sina Peak, is on the border between Kyrgyzstan and Tajikistan.

[20] Bibisara Beishanaliyeva (1926-1973) was the first great Kyrgyz ballerina.

appreciation for the classics, like Chingis Aitmatov[21] People were more concerned with going to bazaars to sell potatoes. Even now, I would be really glad to visit the theater and watch an opera, but I do not have the opportunity.

The woman that I married was my student at the Pedagogical Institute in Osh. She was studying in the philological department, majoring in literature. I was very happy to have that kind of wife —one that I loved. I fell in love with her the first time I saw her. Later, after our marriage, she worked here in Bishkek as the head of the Department of Languages and Literature at the Polytechnic Institute.

I lived with her for 50 years. We had a nice family, consisting of two children. One of them died two years ago and the other one graduated from Bauman University with a "candidate of sciences" degree. He is a good and intelligent person; now he has a wife and a daughter. The point here is love — love for each other, which holds a family together. Family is sacred. It is like alpinism: when you take a step backwards, you fall.

I am not a religious person — I do not practice any religion. However, I trust in God inside of myself. But I consider this a feeling, an internal ingredient, a part of being a person, not a religion.

---

[21] Aitmatov (1928-2008) is Kyrgyzstan's most famous writer.

16. The Beet Farmer

Kaliyjan Januzakova, who is Kyrgyz, was born in 1928 in the village of Ak Bashat, near Kara Balta, Kyrgyzstan. She was a collective farmer. "When I was married, all I did was grow beets on the farm and sell them in the bazaars or exchange them for other goods. I worked as a collective farmer for 20 years," she said. Maksat Annamuradov interviewed her in Ak Bashat on March 20, 2009.

I was born into a family of collective farmers. There were seven children in my family and I was the second oldest. My mother was a housewife; she took care of the children and did the household chores. My father was a collective farmer — specifically, he was a cattle breeder. Life in the village was fine. While we were growing up, we helped our parents around the house and on the farm.

I studied in high school for only four years. After that, I had no choice but to help my family, since World War II had started. It's disappointing, but I have no memory of my time in school, since it was only four years and it was a long time ago. During the war, there were no men in the village, and we — the women — were doing all the duties of the men, like cutting hay on the farms. There was no equipment. Everything was done manually by women.

I remember the Stalin era. Those years were hard and the living conditions were harsh. I think that the war was his responsibility and the human losses were all his fault. I remember when the Turkish people were resettled from the Caucasus to our village[22] — there were around 40 families. However, they were not that friendly and our people had several conflicts

---

[22] Stalin had the Meskhetian Turks deported from the Caucasus in November of 1944 and they arrived in Kyrgyzstan later that year, according to Dr. J. Otto Pohl, an Associate Professor in the International & Comparative Politics Department at the American University of Central Asia, in Bishkek, Kyrgyzstan.

with them. Now none of them are left, since they were not able to live in our village with Kyrgyz people.

I have married two times, since my first marriage was unsuccessful. My first marriage was strongly based in Kyrgyz culture: I had no choice. My parents found me a husband and I never saw him before he became my husband. I lived with him for three years. I was 20 years old when I divorced. I married my second husband when I was 27 years old and I lived with him for 50 years. I had 10 children with him: five daughters and five sons, each of whom got a higher education.

When I was married, all I did was grow beets on the farm and sell them in the bazaars or exchange them for other goods. I worked as a collective farmer for 20 years. Also, there was a factory, Kara Balta Sugar, which used the beets to produce sugar. I sold beets to the factory, too. In the evenings, I would take care of the children, wash clothes, and do other chores. On work days, I woke up at 4 a.m., cleaned the house and made breakfast. Then I sent the cattle to the field and, at 7 a.m., the bus came to take us to the fields. I worked for 12 hours each day in the fields. I was honored several times with medals for my good work.

Back then, women had more self-restraint and were more hardworking. Therefore, women found husbands and had big families and satisfying lives. I did not face problems with raising my children — they are all well-behaved and educated. The secret of having a good, strong family is keeping up a good image of the family in front of the children and showing each other respect and love. Almost everything depends on the parents. My husband and I were examples for our children.

I believe in God, just like almost everybody. I have him in my heart and I negotiate with him when I need him. I consider myself a Muslim. But being strongly religious is not for me because, in the Soviet times, it was not common to practice Islam or any religion. Those were atheistic times. However one of my sons is religious. He practices Islam, visits the mosque every day and reads *namaz* [prays].

Also, our family practices some Muslim cultural traditions, as is usual for every household. For instance, before starting dinner, we always pray to God and thank him for his generosity. Or, whenever we have bad times, we pray to God to help us. Nowadays, we also have Muslim holidays. For instance, since the end of the Soviet era, I have celebrated Orozo [Ramadan]. In addition, during KurmanAit, the family cooks various dishes and thanks God with prayers.

During Soviet times, everybody had their own small farms and cattle, which were sources of food for each household. On the collective farms, we had wheat, which was harvested by the whole village. Also, there were sheds where the cattle were held in the winter. One of my sons now owns one of those sheds.

The government had a bigger role in Soviet times. The collective farms and the agricultural system were controlled. The salaries were paid on time. However, now it is different: the government does not control the rural areas and the farms work independently. Now everybody works for his own household. Before, everything was for the government.

I had no free time when I was young. When I had some free time, I would sleep, since I worked the whole day. However, May 1 was a special day for us. It was Labor Day. That day, I went with a lot of other girls to town and celebrated the holiday by watching the parade. Also, when I was young — and several times when I was in my sixties — I went to Lake Issyk-Kul in the summer.

I am a very patriotic person. I love my country and my town. If I ever had the choice to leave my country for some other country, I would not go. It is my home and my family is here. Some of my children work in Bishkek and other towns in

Kyrgyzstan and I value this from the perspective that they have not forgotten me. They come on holidays and take care of me.

I love to eat and I love our traditional dishes. During the Soviet times, I remember all we were eating was *beshbarmak*, which consists of meat and vegetables with noodles. During the war we had a food shortage, but this was later stabilized and then we, in the rural areas, could get everything we wanted to eat. From what I remember, our national dishes have not changed. The vegetables and the meat for the food we cook were taken from our own farms — we have never gone to the bazaars.

I love to read newspapers and follow the events that take place in Kyrgyzstan. Also, I like to read fairytales and tell them to children. I get a pension and I am satisfied with my life.

17. The Accountant

Mariya Vysockaya, who is Russian, was born in 1933 in the village of Sveltlobovo, in Krasnoyarsk oblast [province], Russia. During World War II, her father and one of her brothers were killed and she and her mother suffered through a famine. When the war ended, her mother moved what was left of the family to Kyrgyzstan, in search of a better life. Nariman Jumayev interviewed her in Bishkek on March 17, 2009.

Our village had about 300 residents. Our family had eight children: five boys and three girls. I was the sixth child. Life was very difficult. My mother told me that, in the year I was born, there was a terrible famine. It was artificially created by the state, she said. [Food] products were selected and taken away in trucks and then simply tossed into a pit. I do not know the exact reasons for this. I assume that it made people hungry and weak, so it was easier to manage them.

Also that year, I was baptized. In our village there was no church so we had to go to another village. There was no persecution because of religion in our village — probably only in the cities. When the war started, I had just started school. There were tears in all the villages when the men were taken to the front. The list came from the district center. My older brothers and my father were taken away on trucks with their belongings.

At the beginning of the war, our *kolkhoz* [collective farm] was good: it had sheep, pigs, horses. A little later, the livestock was slaughtered and taken to the station at Uzhur, which was 90 kilometers away from our village. From there, they were loaded onto trains and sent to the front.

There were people who profited from this by taking more than necessary. And we were hungry. Our students went to the potato fields to harvest and plant. For ourselves, we went to collect the remains of the wheat. It was banned and if they caught you, there was a fine. For adults, they put them in jail. Let the grain be lost, but don't touch it — that was their attitude.

In the spring, when the snow melted, my mom and I went to dig potatoes that had not been collected in the winter and sent to the front. They were already dried. My mom turned them into pancakes.

Also, close to our village was a forest, where we collected *slizun*, which were somewhere between garlic and onions and could be eaten. We also got beets. My mom worked at the time as a security guard. The guards were on duty in pairs and, while one was standing, she would say she had to leave to take care of her business and we would collect beets.

The second problem, after the famine, was disease. I have a sister who caught scrofula — I don't know how — she had big wounds on her head and neck. I got it, too. There was a kind of crust and below it, lice. I would comb until I was bloody, because of the inflammation and pus. I did not know how to deal with the pain. There were no medicines or doctors. To cure me, they stripped all the skin off my neck and then covered it in kerosene.

There was no soap during the war, so my mom, in the old-fashioned way, raked the ash out of the furnace, sifted it, put it in a pot, added boiling water and, with this solution, we washed our heads and our clothes.

During the war, it was very hard. Many died of hunger, but we survived thanks to my mother. When the war was over, one brother was dead and another returned home. My father returned, too, but with inflamed lungs. He soon died.

Then my brother started to work and my life started to

improve. He had friends in Kyrgyzstan, in Tokmak. He resigned from his job and learned to be a driver. Later, my mom said that we would not survive in our village and sent him to Tokmak. After six months, we received a letter from him, so we sold the house, the cow, and the potato harvest, and went to Tokmak. I had just finished the seventh grade.

First we went by train to Novosibirsk. Then we looked and looked and found tickets to Frunze [Bishkek]. From Frunze, we caught the bus to Tokmak. We settled there. With the money from selling our property, we bought land and built a house. I communicated only in Russian, all my life, except for when I lived in Tokmak — then I had to learn a few words of Kyrgyz. I do not remember how long we lived there. Our neighbor left for Frunze and then called for me to come, too.

First, I found work as a *kochegar* [a stoker], then as an assistant painter. Then, I got a job as a dishwasher for the military. After a while, my boss saw that I worked hard and made me a bread cutter. Then I became a waitress, serving generals and officers. I got certificates and awards. At that time, I lived with friends in an apartment. The salary was small, but I tried to save some to buy my mother food. She especially loved red fish.

When I was 23 years old, I met my future husband. He was an officer and I met him where I worked. We married and moved in together. After the birth of our first child, the government gave us an apartment. I left my job and studied to become an accountant. Later, I got a job in that profession and remained there until retirement.

Since my husband was in the military, we got free trips to resorts all over the Soviet Union. Still, we lived on a salary below the national average. I remember, to buy a refrigerator, we had to borrow money. We ate sausages, candy, and other delicacies only on holidays.

18. The Deportee

Sofiya Kim, who is Korean, was born in 1929 in the city of Iman, Russia. Her family was deported to Kazakhstan in 1937, when she was eight. "… People were just hoping that the train wouldn't take them to the concentration camps, which would have meant certain death," she recalled. Later, she and her children moved to Kyrgyzstan. Nariman Jumayev interviewed her in Bishkek on March 15, 2009.

I was born on December 3, 1929 in the village of Iman [Dalnerechensk], near Vladivostok, Russia. I don't remember my childhood well. I just remember that we were poor. In the morning, I had to get up and help my parents. Our land was small — about 700 square meters — and our family had only a couple of cows. I was the oldest of the four children in the family.

In 1937, when I was eight years old, all the Korean people from our village were deported to Kazakhstan because Stalin considered Koreans enemies of the people — i.e., potential allies of fascist Germany — and the enemy must be kept weak.[23]

I cannot remember exactly whether we were warned or not, but I know one thing: we didn't have time to sell anything. We had to leave everything behind: house, cattle, land. We had no money, no belongings, and we were pushed into a train by force — no one told us where it was going.

The interior of the car was simple. We slept on wooden shelves, each one shared by three or four families. The trip took about two weeks and all that time people were just hoping that the train wouldn't take them to the concentration camps, which would have meant certain death. During the long ride, we cooked meals from food we had managed to take with us.

Finally, at some station, the train stopped. We found out

---

[23] In the fall of 1937, Stalin had about 172,000 Koreans deported from the Russian Far East, from the area near the Korean border.

later that the station was called Ush Tobe and was located in Kazakhstan. We saw some mountains and the steppe. We were not given any shelter. For each family, the government had allocated a small plot of land and materials for building a house. While we were building our house, we lived in a hastily constructed dugout.

It was hard to survive, so everybody helped each other. We were provided with some basic food, like flour and corn. Fortunately, nobody in our family died from hunger. The change in climate was a problem. Many children died because of this but, fortunately, in our family, everybody survived. There were no medicines, no doctors, and young babies were dying.

Some years later, World War II began. It didn't have much impact on us: Korean men and women were not taken to the front. We didn't send any food or clothes to the soldiers, either.

When I was 18 years old, I decided to leave my parents' house because I realized that if I stayed in the village, then I would not achieve a lot in my life. I would have to work on the farm and in the fields for my whole life. I did not want that kind of life, so I decided to escape to the town of Kyzyl-Orda. My parents were against it and did not give me permission to go.

My savings, which I had earned by selling rice, were not enough for a ticket, so I had to steal some money from my parents. So, one day, I decided to change my life completely. I took the train to Kyzyl-Orda. Of course, it was somewhat scary, but at the same time I was full of determination and full of hope for a bright future. I went there because I knew that my mother's brother lived there. I did not know his address. I only knew that he worked as the editor of a local Korean newspaper.

It turned out that it was easy to find him. All the Koreans knew him and people showed me where he lived. My uncle accepted me and I stayed there with him. Later, I found a job in a garment factory. It was the only place I could get a job without any education or documents. At the beginning, I was an apprentice but, with time, I became an expert. Sewing turned out to be hard and interesting. Soon, my work began to be noticed, and the management praised me regularly, since I sewed without wasting materials. On holidays, I was regularly given bonuses and I stayed to work in that factory until I retired.

When I was 21, I met my husband. He lived on the same street as me. We had seen each other several times on the street and had gotten acquainted. He was two years older than me and we were considered of suitable ages to be married. His parents knew my uncle well and, therefore, were not opposed to our wedding. But, to register our marriage, I needed documents. So I went to the passport office. I filled out the forms and sent a request to Vladivostok. A month later, I got a positive response and was given a passport.

When we were young, there was not much entertainment. Sometimes a cinema came to our city. Also, we went to the local clubs [community centers], where there were theatrical performances and dances. When I was 22, I gave birth to our first child — a daughter. Then came a son and two more daughters. My husband worked very hard: he was head of the city irrigation service. We communicated mostly with Koreans, but I studied Russian anyway. On the street and at work everybody spoke Russian.

I grew up without getting an education, but I understood that it could provide opportunities in life, so we sent our children to school and then to college. Our son went to work for the irrigation service like his father; our oldest daughter went to technical college; and our two other daughters went to the medical institute. All of them have done very well in their professions.

Our son married and decided to move to Frunze [Bishkek], the capital of the Kyrgyz SSR [Soviet Socialist Republic]. Then our two younger daughters moved there and began to work in clinics. In 1992, my husband and I moved to Kyrgyzstan, too.

Of course, during the Soviet period there was stability and the young people were provided with work. But, at the same time, people were limited in many ways, including financially. Now, our family can afford to buy more things and eat foods that used to be great delicacies.

I have no complaints — every period was good in its own way, including the times of Khruschev and Brezhnev. Of course it is very unfair that the Koreans were repressed and exiled to a foreign country and deprived of shelter and of their property. But, on the other hand, everything turned out okay and my children and grandchildren are living well.

My husband died very early — at 69 — and I was left to live alone. I did not want to live with my children; I decided to live independently. I moved from the house where I had lived with my husband to a nearby apartment, close to my youngest daughter. I spend the whole day in her house. I eat there but sleep at my home.

I can't stand spending much time at home alone, so I visit the activities organized for older people by the Korean Association. Several times a week, elderly Koreans go to the Korean House, where we are provided with tea and bread, sometimes dinner, and gifts on holidays. Musicians play Korean and foreign music. We dance and talk. We are also offered tickets to concerts and performances of Korean artists. We do not pay money for it, only a symbolic membership fee of 25 *som* per month [60 cents]. Everything is sponsored by Korean businessmen.

19. The Farmer

Asel Imankulova, who is Kyrgyz, was born in 1928 in Ak Bashat, a village near Kara Balta, Kyrgyzstan. She worked for much of her life as a collective farmer. "Russian people lived separately from Kyrgyz people, because the Kyrgyz were afraid of the Russians ... When children did not obey their parents, the parents would frighten them by saying that the Russians would come and take them away," she recalled. Maksat Nepesov interviewed her in Ak Bashat on March 20, 2009.

Before I was married, I didn't see anything special. That was the war period, a time of hunger, when my parents worked hard to support our family. I want to say that what I and many people saw at that time — I don't wish it on anybody to see times like that.

During the war, many people did not study — including me. I did not have any opportunity to study, because I was watching my younger siblings. I studied only until the fourth grade. My parents often were not at home and I had to dress and feed the children and send them to school.

My parents worked as farmers and also grew food for themselves. My father worked in the fields and my mother worked in the fields — they grew beets. They worked day and night.

At that time, there were programs, such as building the BCC [Big Chui Canal] to build socialism and that is why my parents were torn away from their children, because they had to fulfill [work] plans and so they had to work day and night.

When my parents weren't around, I had to look after the younger children, so I didn't really have a childhood. I didn't play games. I basically helped around the house, milking cows, dragging buckets of water. I can describe one of the days of my childhood: I woke up at seven in the morning — or, sometimes,

I woke up at six in the morning — and then took care of the children. At the time, my parents didn't let me go anywhere because I was a young girl and it was not decent — it was considered a sign of bad upbringing — for me to go somewhere or go for a walk. In my youth, I basically embroidered things and spun thread. I embroidered clothes for the children with different flowers and ornaments.

I think that our family was strong. Much depends on relationships — from a good, strong word, it sometimes happens that people get angry, but even if someone shouts at you, it is necessary to keep silent and it is necessary to relate to each other warmly, with respect and, of course, love.

Now, in comparison with early times, many things have changed: the roles of the man and the woman in the family — everything has changed. If, in the Soviet period, the man was the head of the family, the supporter of the family, now, on the contrary, in many families, if he has money he spends it on drinking instead of bringing it home to the family. And now women earn more money, save it, and spend it on necessary things.

In my family my parents always worked and on weekends they tried to do all the things around the house that had piled up all week — that was how they rested. Certainly, there were also moments when they drank *kumys* [fermented mare's milk] and played music. But we didn't have entertainment, not like now. Sometimes we would go to see singers or actors who came to the village; they were paid by the collective farm.

We worked a lot in the fields and raised crops, but there were lots of problems, different natural factors and many things that didn't depend on us. If there was a crop, it was good and if there was not, it was bad and we received help from the state. Also, in the Soviet period anything that was necessary — for example, different tinned products — which we could not grow, we could buy with our salaries.

The road to Susamyr and beyond was under construction and, at that time, roads were built by hand. People did everything manually. During that same period, the BCC was also being built. I often went away to help with construction and worked for two to three months.

During the war we did not see any tanks or fighting, but we felt the war. We prepared certain products for the war and, from early childhood, I worked to support the soldiers. We sewed and sent gloves, socks, and butter to the front.

We didn't have enough food. Sometimes we had to skip meals. For example, after harvesting the crops, when there was some wheat left in the fields, we collected it and we wanted to eat it but, since there were children, we gave it to them, instead.

Certainly, sometimes we had good days. For example, when there were holidays, we dressed up, went out walking, feasted, and then went home. From our village, we went to Kara Balta by foot, and that was our entertainment.

The first tractor appeared [in our village] in 1943. Sometimes I drove a tractor myself. Certainly, the arrival of tractors had a strong effect on agriculture. Earlier, people plowed fields with the help of bulls. But with the appearance of tractors, it became easier to plow fields and people had more free time.

I married for love when I was 16 years old. My mother-in-law was a very good person and she treated me kindly, like a daughter. Our village was small and we all knew each other and my future husband knew about me because, in the village, I had a good reputation as a decent young girl. Before we got married, I saw him only five or six times. When we got married, he was 20 years old.

Let me tell you about our food: in the 50s and 60s and, in general, after World War II, we ate *manty, lagman,* and *beshbar-*

mak.²⁴ Now everyone eats with dishes and salads and so on. Earlier, we simply fried meat and put it on two plates on the table. Now all the products we have, we grow ourselves and store in cellars and sometimes, when we don't have anything, we go to the market. Earlier, food was more delicious and nutritious than now — for example, now we make lagman from leftover meat — and when we ate it we had much more energy than, for example, my daughter-in-law does now.

By religion, I'm a Muslim. I believe in God, but I don't pray and never go to mosque, because I am already old and it is hard for me to move. But, in my family I have people who do all these things. My grandson prays and goes to mosque. I think it's good, because people who pray will never begin to drink and smoke, and alcoholism and smoking are serious problems now, especially among youth. When I was young, I did not know anybody who prayed, because in the Soviet period, there was no time for that. We had cattle and other matters that we had to take care of from morning until evening.

I speak one language: Kyrgyz. I know a little Russian but I can't speak it. It was not necessary for me to learn it, because all the people around me spoke Kyrgyz so there was no need to learn another language. Russian people lived separately from Kyrgyz people, because the Kyrgyz were afraid of the Russians. We were afraid because, in 1916, during World War I, Russians collected people to serve as soldiers for the war. In Kyrgyzstan, from the Chui and Issyk-Kul areas, everyone ran away to China.²⁵ This stayed in the people's mentality and they

---

²⁴ *Manty* are steamed dumplings filled with meat; *lagman*, is a dish made from noodles topped with chopped meat and vegetables and covered in a savory sauce; *beshbarmak* consists of boiled, sliced meat — usually mutton — and noodles.

²⁵ This refers to the events known as Urkun: In 1916, during World War I, when the Tsarist Russian government tried to conscript Central Asians into its army, the Kyrygz rose up and resisted and thousands of them fled to China. Estimates of the Kyrgyz death toll range from 3,000 to 100,000.

were afraid of Russians until World War II or even longer. When children did not obey their parents, their parents would frighten them by saying that the Russians would come and take them away. Russians grew tomatoes and when they ate them, people said that they drank blood. Now we have mixed and got used to each other.

My husband died 20 years ago [in 1989]. I have three children: two daughters and one son. My oldest daughter lives in Tokmok and she already has a husband and children. My second daughter lives in Kara Balta. And, my son, by tradition, lives with me, because he is my only son. He has four children: two girls and two boys. He also has a tractor and uses it to harvest hay, which is the basic source of income for the family.

And now, times have became more difficult. The pension at the present time is 1,200 *som* [per month — about $28]. That is very little. It's not even enough for a bag of flour, which costs 1,500 *som*. I grow many products myself, but the things that I do not grow, I have to buy at the market. My basic income comes from my children, but sometimes it happens that they don't have money. My pension is so small that it is not enough for medicine and medical treatment. After all, I'm already old, and I have health problems. I have a limp and I think it is because I spent a lot of time standing. For about 15 years, I worked as a milkmaid and went around in rubber boots and dragged buckets of milk. It is very insulting for me that in my youth I worked for the good of the state and now they give me such a small pension.

20. THE JANITOR

Tokon Rakhmanova, who is Kyrgyz, was born in 1940 in the village of Ak Bashat [Sosnovka], near Kara Balta, Kyrgyzstan. She worked as a farmer and then as a janitor. "The concept of love was not widespread in our time. By tradition, our parents married us. If we disobeyed our parents, it was considered shameful for our family," she said. Azat Nepesov interviewed her in Ak Bashat on March 15, 2009.

There was no school in our village. We went to the next village to study. It was a long way; it took a lot of time to walk there. That's why I finished only four grades. After that, I was needed at home. The post-war years were very difficult. A lot of husbands and sons did not return from the front. Each village felt the shortage of men's hands. I helped my parents watch the children and run the household.

My father was a stockbreeder and I often helped him when I was a child. We raised *karakurt* sheep and often took them to pasture in Talas and Susamyr. He died when he was 62 years old. My mother worked for most of her life in the beet fields and died when she was 72 years old. They had 10 children, including me, and three of them have died.

My parents were strict when I was growing up — and it wasn't only my parents. Back then, we didn't go to concerts, to the cinema, or to other cultural events. Our only entertainment was playing games with the neighborhood children. There were three very popular games: *altyn-baka*,[26] *joluk samay*,[27] and *shakek samay*.[28] I married early and, after that, I didn't have any free time, since I was always occupied with my children and my family life.

---

[26] A swing for two people.

[27] In this game, one child hides a scarf and others try to find it.

[28] In this game, one of a group of children hides a ring in his hand, and another child has to guess where the ring is.

My native language is Kyrgyz, but I know a little bit of Russian. I had to learn it when I worked as a milkmaid, because many of my colleagues were Russian. At that time, many people aspired to learn Russian, but since I am not educated, I could not learn Russian well. Besides, the people around me communicated only in Kyrgyz. I would like to know Russian because, when you go to the city or the market or the hospital, Russian is necessary.

I am religious. I am a Muslim. I pray and I go to mosque. I read the Koran and do *davat*.[29] One of the duties of adults is to teach children basic Islamic principles. In the Soviet period, there were no mosques — I did not go to mosque. But my parents prayed at home. When I was young, I did not pray. I started to pray only in the past two years or so.

In the Soviet period, Islam did not spread for two reasons. First, we were allowed to have only one religion: Communism. Muslims were despised and sometimes even pursued as enemies. Therefore, practically everyone conducted their religious affairs at home, where no one could see. Second, we did not have enough time. I mean we physically did not have time. We spent all day in the fields.

I remember when the first TV arrived in our village. It was 1965. When I first saw it, I was surprised. But I liked to watch concerts and Indian movies and, because of these interesting programs, I began to watch TV. But I still like to do embroidery better — it is my favorite form of entertainment.

During the war, I was small, so I don't remember much. I remember only that I was sent to the field to work as a shepherd. All our people hated Germans and when they talked about the war, they always said: "We should exterminate them!" Why was there so much rage? Because we lost so much in the war. Many people lost family members. In each family

---

[29] Also known as *"da'wah,"* it is essentially missionary work — "inviting" people to Islam.

there were funerals. Also, we had never seen Germans and that is part of why we hated them so much.

I remember when Stalin died in 1953. We learned about it from the radio. There was a solar eclipse that day and everyone was frightened and sat silently. Many people thought the eclipse was directly connected with the loss of their great leader. It was a big loss. From what I remember, there were three days of mourning. Nobody worked or went to school. Many people cried. Then, Khrushchev came next. The only thing I remember about the Khrushchev era was that sometimes there was famine because of poor harvests — and then there was no bread. Khrushchev has a bit of a negative association for me.

I never wanted to live in the city. I like it here [in the village] with my relatives. Besides, without an education and without speaking Russian, there aren't many opportunities for me in the city. Certainly, I have gone with my relatives to large cities for concerts and such, but I never had a desire to stay. I believe one's older years should be spent at home.

The concept of love was not widespread in our time. By tradition, our parents married us. If we disobeyed our parents, it was considered shameful for our family. Anyway, I married.

My husband worked on a collective farm as a foreman. Later he worked as the supply manager at a school. He died in 1985, when he was 52 years old. I have grandsons now. One of them left for Ireland recently and he sends us money.

I worked as a janitor at a school for 25 years. I also worked on a beet farm and as a milkmaid. At that time, the state really supported us. There were never shortages of drinking water, irrigation water, or harvesting equipment — the collective farm provided everything.

After we became an independent country, the collective farms were broken up and the land was distributed to individuals. Now there are four farms in our village. It was better when there was one big collective farm. Now we cannot hope for any help from the state. Everything depends on us. Being involved in farming and stockbreeding has become very risky. There are problems with the irrigation system and there is an acute shortage of fertilizers and other materials.

Productivity fell sharply after independence. There was hunger. People lived in fear. We did not know what would happen the next day or the day after. We were not divided into rich people and poor people; before the 1990s, everyone was equal. But from the first years of independence, there were rich men who had appropriated the land and equipment of the Soviet Union.

We all still grow things like cucumbers, tomatoes, carrots, and other vegetables, just as we did in the Soviet days. Sometimes it is necessary to go to the market to buy something. My favorite dish is *beshbarmak*. I also like Uzbek dishes like *lagman* and *manty*. People used to drink *bozo*, which is prepared from corn and is a little bit alcoholic. Back then, people did not drink alcohol the way they do now.

Now, because of unemployment, many young people leave the country to find work in other countries. Unemployment has created problems in the village like alcoholism and hopelessness. So the young people hear that someone has left and earned a lot of money and then they leave, too. They frequently come back sad. Some of them even regret leaving their parents and their homes to earn small sums of money.

It used to be that the man was the head of the family and everything depended on him. Now the roles have changed a little and women are more active. The woman now goes to the market more, manages things more — basically the woman is in charge of the household finances.

This change is related to the fact that many men have left

to work abroad, so now women have to perform men's duties. Those men who remain here are often alcoholics.

21. The Tractor Driver

Ilhomjan Karimov,[30] who is Uzbek, was born in 1924 in the village of Bazar Korgan in the Jalal-Abad [province] of Kyrgyzstan. He worked as a tractor driver. "During collectivization, two people from the government came to Bazar Korgan ... At that time, no one knew anything about collectivization and some people were against it and they beat up the two government people with stones," he recalled. Abdurahman Aripov interviewed him in Bazar Korgan on March 10, 2009.

When I was a kid, before the war, we lived like middle-class people — not poor and not so rich. We didn't have a farm and none of our family members farmed. During the hard times, everyone suffered alike.

I went to school for only three and a half years, because of the war. Most of my classmates and my teachers died in the war. The teachers were the first people taken to war — they went as commanders. Most of them didn't come back. Kamoldin [one of the teachers] and some other teachers came back from war, though.

I wasn't interested in education. I didn't have a favorite class. I never dreamed of getting a higher education and becoming some important person. At school we usually copied down everything written on the blackboard and listened to the teacher. And after going home, we did some homework. That's all we did at school.

We studied in our native language at school. We had almost no Russian classes. I almost always spoke Uzbek, because it is my native language. Then Russian people started sending us equipment and I became a tractor driver. And with the Russians I used to speak Russian and with the Uzbeks, Uzbek. And soon, the Russians learned to speak Uzbek, too.

---

[30] Not his real name. He asked that his name not be used, to maintain his privacy.

In my childhood, with my friends, I played "nuts." We used to throw nuts at one another on the ground. And if I hit it, I took both — mine and the other one, which I won. Also, we played a game called *eshak mindi* where we used to jump over each other. One person was standing, bending over, and we jumped over him.

Then I began gambling. Once, after I got involved in gambling, my mom heated a small coin on the fire and put it in my hand and asked me if I would gamble anymore. I cried, "I will not gamble, I will not gamble!" After that, I stopped playing games for money.

At night, our grandmothers told us fairytales and stories. They also told us about TV, which could show us what was going on in other parts of the world. The first TVs came to our village in the beginning of the 1960s and we gathered at people's houses and watched TV together.

I didn't go to the war and I didn't fight; I worked as a tractor driver. Young people were taken to the war. Old people were taken into work battalions to fix old broken railways. Children were taken to Toshkumir [a small coal-mining city].

The war had very bad effects on our lives. There was a big problem with food; getting food was hard. People were starving. And most of the people who left for the war didn't come back. Those who did return, came back wounded and sick.

Our village, Bazar Korgan, changed a lot. Almost everybody was sent to the war and those who weren't, were sent to the mines. There was no one left to farm. We were starving, there was no food. Only a few tractor drivers were left in the village and we farmed everything. We planted and grew food for people. It was a difficult time. Sometimes we boiled grass and ate it.

There was no salt in the village. People got fat because of that. Everybody experienced problems with their weight because of the lack of salt. However, there was salt brought from Toktogul by people on donkeys. It was then crushed into small pieces and sold for very high prices. It was like that. Then the mulberries ripened and we ate them and waited for the wheat to ripen. But we couldn't wait until it was fully ripe. We used to cook half-ripe wheat and eat it. We walked without shoes. Our feet were sore and, after that, we made shoes out of leather. We survived somehow.

Many people were resettled here. Many people moved here and many moved from here. Rich people were forced to move to Azerbaijan — our grandparents had to leave. And some of them were forced to move to the suburbs of Tashkent, to a village called Kovunchi.

During collectivization, two people from the government came to Bazar Korgan. A guy called Bematov, who had a gun, and another guy, a Tatar, came and told everyone about collectivization. At that time, no one knew anything about collectivization and some people were against it and they beat the two government people with stones. They were half-dead but didn't die.

My friends and I saw the big crowd surrounding the government men. It was near Taylak Ata [a small cafe where old people gather, in the center of Bazar Korgan, near the central mosque]. We went over and saw that one of the people was dying — suffering and shaking on the ground. At that moment, a person with his face covered came over with a knife and took his head. The two men were buried in a cemetery not far from the center.

Later, the government people who were elected tried to collectivize us. Some people were against it, but they were taken at night from their houses and sent to Osh and imprisoned. And, after that, everything was collectivized. Everyone worked. I worked with my father, growing cotton.

My father and I used to take all the cotton in a big cart to be weighed. There was a person, a receiver, who weighed all the cotton and, after weighing it, gave a signed paper for you to take to the cashier, who would give you money. The cashier sat near the gates with piles of money. And, next to him, there was a store that sold everything: sugar, candies, clothes, shoes.

If anyone had anything, it was collected for common use. If I had a cart, I would give it up and if you had something, you would give it up. And so, in this way, collectivization was established in our village. Before people got used to collectivization, life was difficult. But after everyone got used to it, everything was fine.

We got our salaries according to how much we worked. We had to submit a paper to get our salaries. Our roads here were in very bad condition and we were forced to fix roads ourselves, manually, by putting gravel in the holes. After we fixed the roads, a person would sign our paper and we could get our salaries.

I am a Muslim. My parents always said that there is only one God and that we have to pray five times a day. So I just follow their religion and do what they taught me. During Soviet times, though, the government put a lot of pressure on religious people. Many mosques were closed and we used hide at home or in the fields to pray. During Ramadan and other Muslim holidays, we had to pray in the fields, too. If we were caught, our own Uzbeks would punish us for praying and being religious.

There were several old mosques in our village, but all of them were closed and we couldn't enter them. One of them became a garage and, after that, it became a cotton plant, but now it is open again. We couldn't fast back then, either. At school, I remember, our teacher forced us to eat and drink during class so that we couldn't fast. We tried to fast in a hidden way, without letting anyone know. Now, as you see, I can easily go and pray and fast whenever I want, without any fear. Back then, people could study religion in many cities, like Bukhara, which had some of the best religious teachers. They studied at night, gathering secretly at someone's house. But no one from my family ever studied there.

My favorite food was *osh* [*plov* — rice pilaf]. The way people make food has changed a lot since my childhood. Now it tastes much better and we can make whatever we want. Before, *osh* was made from other grains, not rice. People almost didn't eat *osh* at all during the war. These days, no one makes *osh* like they used to. Nowadays, life is better — you can buy everything from markets and make whatever you want.

As you can see, nowadays we don't even eat bread that was made couple of days earlier — we eat fresh bread. But during the war we ate anything we could get. Before, a rich person could afford everything he wanted and a poor person couldn't get many of the things he wanted. Sometimes, during the difficult times, we didn't even get bread. Now we have new foods, like *lagman* and *kabob*s, which came from other nations.

After the fall of the Soviet Union, everybody got land from the government, but some people don't want to work hard at farming. Those who can work well and have some knowledge go abroad and work there. As you see, there are a lot people building huge houses and buying expensive cars. All of these things were bought with money sent from abroad. These people working abroad are helpful for our country. People can afford many things because of them. They pay for weddings and parties with money sent from abroad.

22. The KGB Agent

Komiljan Djurabekov was born in 1928 in the village of Bazar Korgan, near Jalal-Abad, Kyrgyzstan. He lived there until he left for the army. Later, he studied in a "political school" in Tashkent and then worked for the KGB. Abdurahman Aripov interviewed him in Bishkek on March 22, 2009.

Nomadic people never had a government. They never stayed in one place, because they were nomadic. They moved from place to place, finding grass for their livestock. Nomadic people didn't have nationalities, either — they were identified by where they were from and only after that, by their names. Chingis Khan didn't have a government, because he was nomadic, too. And that's why, after the October Revolution, the goal was to establish a government in Central Asia. The goal was to make people live somewhere and divide them up, to make it easier to control them.

After the revolution, people were divided into ethnic groups, and that's why the Kyrgyz, Uzbek, Tajik, Turkmen, and Kazakh SSRs [Soviet Socialist Republics] were created. It was called "delimitation by nationality." And all that was done in order to make it easier to exercise power over the people of Central Asia. When all nationalities are the same nationality, they are difficult to control. And people can just refuse to obey the government. When people are broken up into small countries, they are easier to control.

Just like the Russian Empire, the Bolsheviks established this kind of government. All orders came from Moscow. With the construction of railroads, schools, and hospitals, they began transmitting their culture to Central Asia. But Central Asian culture was a Muslim culture. And it was a Christian culture that came here. That's why Lenin was always saying that the "suburbs" of Russia should be better supplied than the central regions: in order to raise some interest there; in order to convince them that, "We are supporting them, so they should respect us."

And, like this, a country was created. And that's why many nationalists were killed in 1937 — so that they wouldn't think about making their own governments. At that time, Akram Ikramov and Fayzulla Hodjaev, people involved in the Uzbek revolution, were killed as nationalists.

All the laws and rules were made in Moscow and were sent to the other republics. And there the laws were copied. And that's how the Soviet Empire was established. The Soviet Union was an empire, too — a huge empire. Because of the richness of its lands, it became very strong. It never adopted capitalism and wasn't ruled by capitalists. The USSR, independently provided food for itself and also exported food to other countries, to draw them closer.

The worst system that has ever been created is government. Governmental institutions work only for themselves. They transmit their ideas through television. For older people, they have serials [multi-part movies]. For youth, they made up different shows and concerts. They don't think about the essentials. They forget about them. And they create, instead, an illusion — a circus.

World War II had a very bad effect on us. It was the most bloody war that has ever been fought. And a lot of money and goods were spent on it. It was a destructive war. This war was begun by financial magnates, not by Hitler. Hitler was just told that German people should live better and that's why he needed to conquer other countries. And Hitler was told that, for a better life, he needed more land.

It was rooted in the fact that politicians were afraid of the USSR, because the political and economic structure of the USSR wasn't convenient for the capitalists. So they began to conquer the USSR. I don't know how many people from Kyrgyzstan died, but I can say a lot of people died. Maybe, out of all the people who were mobilized, only 10 percent came back and the other 90 percent died. And we suffered after the war. We didn't recover for a long time.

The most punishable crime in USSR was the killing of innocent people; the second was corruption and taking bribes; the third one was "speculation" [running a private business]. People dealing in gold were punished severely, too: they were sentenced to be shot.

I worked here [in Bishkek] when a struggle against illegal trading began. Those who were doing business were punished severely. This was in a Bishkek factory — a knitting factory. Near that [government] factory, another one was illegally built, which wasn't on the government's books. It produced all the same products that were produced in the legal factory. And they were sent to stores and shops all over. The profits were divided among the people who created the illegal business. A lot of this money was also given to people in high positions. They knew about this illegal business but didn't take any action against it.

All that happened in 1959. It was called "The Knitting Factory Incident." It was a famous court trial in the USSR. Several prosecutors were imprisoned, several lawyers, two people from the *obmin* [state government], and several people from the central committee of the Kyrgyz SSR. Razzakov[31] was forced to leave his post. Seven people were sentenced to death. Two of them died in prison because of heart disease and the

---

[31] Iskhak Razzakovich Razzakov (1910-1979), was raised in an orphanage. He went to university in Moscow and then returned to Central Asia to work in the Uzbek government's planning committee where he soon became chairman. From 1945 to 1950 he served as Chairman of the Council of Ministers of what was then the Kyrgyz Soviet Socialist Republic (SSR). From 1950 to 1961, he served as First Secretary of the Central Committee of the Communist Party of the Kyrgyz SSR.

rest were shot. Many others were imprisoned or sent to different "colonies." Most of them didn't come back

Although there wasn't much immigration here, some Jewish and Caucasian people did come to live here. Some Chechen people who were enemies of the Soviet Union also came.[32]

During the war they all worked here and, after the war, they were allowed to go back. They lived and worked here and no one had anything against them. They were treated like equal citizens of the country. The local people did not discriminate against them. After the war, the Jewish people left fast. But the Chechen people left slowly. The last Chechen person probably left Bazar Korgan in 1955 or 1956.

During World War II, there was a [ration] card system. Cards were given to everyone. Everybody got about a half a kilogram of bread every day. We got the bread from stores by showing our cards. Almost no one died from hunger during World War II. But during the famine in 1933, many people had died because of a lack of food.

At that time, all over the world, there was dry weather and a lack of water. In 1933, almost everything that grew dried up and died. Everything stopped growing. There was almost no food. And people ate everything they could find. We ate dogs and dead animals. At that time, many migrants came to our region from Kazakhstan. A lot of Kazakhs came to our region on their camels. And the camel would be standing there alive, but the owner of the camel would be falling down and almost dying of hunger. I don't know why they didn't eat their camels.

My father had land before collectivization. I was a little kid at that time and my father was given a hectare of land. We planted cotton there; others planted vegetables and other kinds of plants on their land. We gave all the cotton we grew to the

---

[32] Stalin had all the Chechens deported from Chechnya to Kazakhstan and Kyrgyzstan on 23-29 February of 1944.

Pakhta Abat cotton factory and the factory gave us money for it.

Collectivization began in Bazar Korgan during the hunger years — in about 1933. Theoretically, collectivization was right and it was good that the harvest went to the government and the government paid the farmers. But collectivization is not a productive way of doing something. Everyone works differently. Some work pretty well, but others do a poor job.

Religion was mostly prohibited in the USSR, because religion just distracts you from your job. Besides, believing in God won't make you any money. And if you pray to God and ask him to give you money, he will not give it to you. You have to work to earn your money.

Before, all the mullahs and imams were rich. They got part of the income of each farm and of each stockbreeder. So the USSR prohibited mass religious meetings and closed all the madrassas and mosques. They didn't want people to go and pray five times a day. It takes a lot of time to pray. And also they say that a mosque is God's house, but everybody knows that in the Koran and in the Bible it is said that God has no home.

Then why do people go to mosques? In order to ask for help or for something they need from God. God doesn't need our prayers. Let's take an example: We hold a memorial ceremony 40 days after someone's death and then, again, one year later. Who needs these memorials? Does God or the dead person need them? No. They are held in order to show other people that we honor the dead, to show that we remember those who are close to us. And here a person honors his close people by sacrificing a sheep or a cow. And that is all done for appearances.

Here is a story: There was a Kyrgyz person who was walking and he met another Kyrgyz person. The first one says, "Hey, Umurzak, have you heard that someone died?" And the other asks, "What did they sacrifice?" And the first one answers: "A cow." And Umurzak says, "Well then I won't go — he was that kind of person." But if a horse was sacrificed [which would be considered more delicious], then that Kyrgyz person would go and eat horse meat and say good stuff about the dead person.

When I was a child, we read and wrote in the Latin alphabet. In 1935-1936, when I went to first grade, there was only one teacher. He taught us everything — math, algebra, and foreign languages. It was only later that we got many teachers and each of them taught one subject. When the war began, all the teachers were sent to war immediately. Real school and real education only began again after the war.

As for me, I finished only four years of school because of the war. I have only four years of education. After the war, I went to serve in the army — in the army, you also get educated — and it was there that I studied. Studying depends on the person himself: if you want to get an education, you can do it even without a teacher.

After I came back from the army, I was given a leadership position. I had four years of education and I became the director of a dormitory. It was because I came back from the army as a Party member. After a year, I was chosen as a member of the district committee. Also, I worked as a Party worker and as vice president of the department. Then I graduated from a Party school that was a branch of a party school in Moscow.

My native language is Uzbek. It is my language from my mother's side because my mom kept me inside herself for about nine months and then gave a birth to me. She also raised me. There are families where the father comes home and sees his child only once a month and all the rest of the time, my mother educated me and raised me. But still, your father is the closest person to you. Why, you ask? Because the seed came from him.

I know many Turkic languages, because they are all similar. I also know Russian, because, in the army, people spoke Russian and I learned Russian. The Party school was also in Russian.

Electrification began in our region probably during the war or maybe at the beginning of the war. There is a small village not far from Bazar Korgan. It is called Sovietskaya. And there, on the river, the first small hydroelectric station was built. People accepted electricity as a gift from God. Everything is moved by energy. And the cheapest energy comes from hydroelectric plants. Thermoelectric power stations are not very profitable. They require gas and coal.

23. The Opium Farmer & Her Husband

Sulayka (Asanbayeva) Arpachieva, who is Kyrgyz, was born in 1951 in the village of Jeti Oguz, on the south shore of Lake Issyk-Kul, in Kyrgyzstan. Her family raised opium for a collective farm. Karagul Arpachiyev, who is also Kyrgyz, was born in 1951 in the village of Konurolon, in the Tomsk district of Issyk-Kul oblast [province], in Kyrgyzstan. They were married in 1973. Dovlet Hojamuradov and Gulzara Hayytmuradova interviewed them in the city of Karakol, on March 15, 2009.

Mrs. Sulayka (Asanbayeva) Arpachieva

I had four sisters and four brothers. We lost two of them recently. Our parents are also not with us in this world any more. My father went to World War II in 1941 and returned injured in 1944. After his return, our family was enlarged by another son.

Our family planted, raised, and gathered opium.[33] Starting in May, we would work in the fields, weeding. The collective farm gave people sections of opium fields to weed. So our summer vacations were spent in the fields, weeding. It wasn't until the sixth grade that we were allowed to cut the opium. The opium needs to be cut before sunrise, when the weather is still cool. So we would take our equipment and go to the fields at 4 a.m. We would cut the opium and give it to the collective farm, which would pay us. We'd spend the money for clothing and school supplies in September.

I was in high school in the 1960s. During my school years,

---

[33] According to Jenishbek Nazaraliev's 2003 book *Fatal Red Poppies*, (Medical Press: Moscow), opium poppies were grown in Kyrgyzstan during World War II as a way to get morphine for military hospitals. After the war, cultivation continued until 1974. Kyrgyzstan used to produce 16 percent of the world's opium.

we would spend a lot of time in our village's library. We loved to read books by Kyrgyz writers like Togulbay Sadyrbekov, Timirkul Umetaliyev, and Chingis Aitmatov. Their books are about the lives and fates of Kyrgyz people. We didn't read classics by authors like [Alexandre] Dumas as much, because we could understand only a little Russian.[34]

There was only one club [community center] in the village and we would watch movies there occasionally. The movies were usually Kyrgyz films or films about World War II. We hated the idea of anything German because of what we saw in the movies. Now our perceptions about Germans have changed. Now we think differently. We had a lot of Germans living in our village. Also, there were Tatars Uyghurs, Uzbeks, [Meskhetian] Turks, and Dungans — they all lived with us in peace. We adopted their cultures and dishes and they adopted ours.

We don't remember the period of Stalin, for we were small then. We remember the periods of Khrushchev and Brezhnev better. We baked bread from moldy barley and corn during Khrushchev's rule. That bread was not as healthy as the regular bread from wheat. In those times, ideology was strong, but there was no wheat. People were calmed with the promises that everything was going to get better soon. They lacked sugar and other things, but they survived.

During the Brezhnev period, conditions got better. We had flour and sugar in the stores, but there still were products which were scarce. In the schools we read Brezhnev's writings, like *Malaya Zemlya* [*Small World*], where he said "If there is bread then there is song." We had no foreign products in those years. Later, we found out that it was in the government's interest to sell us its own products. For example, Soviet cars were not in demand, because of competition. We didn't import foreign goods — we only exported.

---

[34] Although Dumas was, of course, French, his books had not been translated into Kyrgyz, so they were available to Asanbayeva only in Russian.

In our free time, we would go the movies. The cinemas had long lines and were full of young people all the time. There were only two cinemas in Karakol: one was named Mir and the other, Issyk-Kul. Now everyone has DVD players and there are no lines at the cinemas.

I think the government made a big mistake by suppressing religion. We were exposed to atheistic values starting in school. Traditions like fasting during Orozo Ait [Ramadan] were not acceptable. Only older people would fast and almost no one prayed. Now even young people fast and pray. Nevertheless, people held onto rituals like circumcisions and weddings. But still, we had incidents when people in high positions could not come to the funerals of their parents.

The influence of the Party on its members was strong. When our grandmother passed away we were going to hold a traditional Kyrgyz funeral, but when the Third Secretary of the Regional Government found out, our uncle told us we had to simplify the event, which meant not doing it according to Kyrgyz traditions. Lots of people lost their positions because of religion. That was one of the failures of the Soviet government. It frustrated people; it was very hard.

In addition, it was decided that the Russians would get all the top positions. The youth objected and many young people were injured or even killed during the protest. I think that those kinds of events eroded the government's legitimacy. And then certain actions were taken, like the separation of the Baltic states from the Soviet Union.

In 1968, my parents decided I should continue my education by studying at the Mayakovskiy Institute [now Arabayeva University in Bishkek]. I didn't pass the exams, though, and returned home crying. Back then, it was not acceptable for young people not to have jobs, so my parents sent me to Karakol to study to be an accountant.

The next year, I received my accounting certificate. My parents decided I should get a higher education so I applied to the Karakol Pedagogical Institute and was accepted into the Department of Mathematics and that's where I met my future husband. Our student years were fun and interesting. We got stipends of 28 *ruble*s [a month], which was enough for food and clothing and we lived in the dormitory. I finished the first year with all 5s [As].

During our university years, for entertainment, we would go to the movies. But we would only go after exams, because we couldn't afford to spend too much because we were on our own and our parents weren't able to support us financially. There weren't any really rich people during the Soviet era. Everyone was equal back then. If someone had a second car, he would be asked where he had found the money for it. Those who spent more than others were caught and locked up in jail.

Later, I got the Lenin stipend, which was 90 *ruble*s. Still, we would not go to restaurants except on special occasions. We ate in cafeterias. We did everything ourselves in those days. These days, students get good grades in the universities by paying [bribing], not by studying hard. There was no bribing when we were in the university. Now education has lost the quality it used to have. Although the city schools do offer some sort of education, the village schools provide only a low level of education — almost no education — since there is a shortage of teachers in rural areas.

We married after we graduated from the university. The authorities told people where to work back then. So I was sent to the Aksuy *rayon* [county] and my husband was sent to Osh province. We appealed to the ministry, asking it to send us both to the same place: Aksuy. I started teaching and reached the "high category" of teachers at that school.

Women only got a month of vacation when they were pregnant back then. So, after I gave birth, my husband's younger brother helped me take care of the kids. Every day, I would feed the kids and then go to my job and my brother-in-law would care for them.

My youngest daughter was born in 1985 and that was the year when the authorities banned the practice of putting kids in *beshik*s [cradles]. It was found that it was unhealthy. There were nurses who went house to house and made sure that people were not using cradles. So, for the first time, we had to buy a baby carriage.

Mr. Karagul Arpachiyev

My father was not an educated person. He worked on a collective farm. My mother died when I was six years old and my younger brother was two and my sister was nine months. So our childhood was very hard. Our grandmother took care of us. The 1950s and 1960s were difficult periods for everyone, since the post-war reconstruction was still going on. People suffered materially and socially.

Our father was only able to bring us up with the help of our grandmother. We did chores every day — we prepared firewood and fed livestock — so we never had time to play with our peers. I also took care of my younger siblings. Our grandmother would come and take care of us, helping my father, who worked on the collective farm. My father was busy with irrigation, harvesting, and other chores of that kind.

Each province had its own agricultural specialization. For instance, Osh was busy with cotton and tobacco. Talas was known for potatoes, wheat, and beans. Chui grew corn, squash, wheat, and rye. Issykul focused on fruits like apples of different types, cherry-plums, cherries, and so on. One good thing about agriculture in the Soviet era was the way they tried to preserve the productivity of our arable lands. Nowadays, this is a problem because of privatization.

We did well in school. Our childhood had a big influence on that. We were brought up with a hardworking attitude. The challenges we experienced in our childhood boosted our desire to study seriously. We moved toward our goals persistently and never left anything unfinished. So all of my siblings took their studies seriously and did well in school.

Our father married another woman. So we had another eight siblings in our family. So that made 11 of us. Overall, I grew up in a good family, where everyone got a higher education and now holds a respectable job.

The good life we are all living did not come easily. We faced challenges when our parents passed away, before our younger brothers were properly established. So it fell on the eldest siblings to finish the job that our parents had not been able to finish: marrying off our brothers and helping them financially until they could stand on their own. With their efforts and our help, we got over those challenges. We had a shortage of food and clothing. Nevertheless, we were able to take care of our brothers and gave them a good start in life. We were able to do that without any help from anyone in our village.

My wife and I started studying at the Pedagogical Institute in Karakol [Kyrgyzstan] in 1969. We studied in the Department of Mathematics and that's where we met. We graduated in 1973 and then got married. Then we went to the village of Tepke in the Aksuy region. That's when the second chapter of our lives began. That chapter was all about our family and the challenges I faced while fulfilling my responsibilities to my family. Raising my children and giving them opportunities in life was my primary responsibility and I have accomplished it so far.

When we had children, we moved to Karakol. I think it was the right decision because the city provided better educational opportunities for our children. To give our children a good education was one of our primary responsibilities as parents. Once we moved, I started working at the Pedagogical Institute and my wife was able to get a job at the Toktogul Lyceum. We worked at the Institute and the Lyceum until we retired.

At this stage of my life, I do not regret the problems I faced throughout my life. This kind of life gave me good experiences and made me strong enough to face any challenge. My life path was a good lesson and it was motivation for my children to help each other in the future. When I was a child, I wished that someone would help us take care of our siblings so that I could have some fun playing with my peers. This taught me to help people.

Although we were just teachers, we were able to take care of our children. There is a custom among Kyrgyz people of inviting the bride's family members and giving them presents. My wife and I were able to afford to do that on our own. Now our children are independent and doing well. So I think we deserve to enjoy our senior years.

24. THE SHEPHERD & HIS WIFE

Dogdurbai Kachikeev, who is Kyrgyz, was born in 1931 in the city of Karakol, on the east end of Lake Issyk-Kul, in Kyrgyzstan. He is a shepherd, from a family of shepherds. Kashymkan Kachikeeva, who is also Kyrgyz, was born in 1932 in the village of Munduz, Kyrgyzstan. They married in 1949. Dovlet Hojamuradov and Gulzara Hayytmuradova interviewed them in the city of Karakol on March 15, 2009.

Mr. Dogdurbai Kachikeev

I was born in the 1930s. Back then, people did not keep track of time accurately. My mom used to say that the official data was always off by at least one year. We had a neighbor who worked as the head of the passport agency. She made passports for us. So whatever dates we needed, we named, and she could work it out and bring the passports to us. Lots of people changed their dates of birth to skip the army or to get benefits like early pensions.

My childhood was harsh. There was a famine and times were bad and we cried. For meals, we would drink one spoonful of *talkan* [ground grain] mixed into one *piala* [bowl] of tea. We would eat potatoes from time to time. Also, we would eat dried peaches from time to time. Our elders were shepherds. We were young and didn't know how to do that work, so we worked in the city [Karakol]. We started working at five or six. We worked long days and nights.

I took evening classes. The way I learned was through reading newspapers and writing on them. For example, I would read the paper and then practice writing on it, on the corner. That's how I learned and became a little bit literate. I didn't have a pen, so I dipped a big thorn in ink to write. I took what I had written to the teacher of my evening classes and asked him to check it. He showed me my mistakes and commented on what I had done correctly. I wrote and read every day. I finished five grades, officially.

Evening school was serious. If we didn't come to class, they asked us where we were. They would punish us if we were late or if we skipped classes. The punishment could be the loss of an entire [monthly] salary [from the collective farm], or even jail.

World War II did not touch Central Asia directly. But we helped the war effort by making socks and coats and by harvesting wheat and sending it to the front. This resulted in a scarcity of clothing and food here in Central Asia. And there were lots of sick people — kids especially. There was an epidemic of typhus. Ten to 20 people died and they were buried in their clothing because there was nothing else to wrap them in. I saw it with my own eyes.

My parents were shepherds. My relatives are shepherds. When I was young, I worked on the collective farm as a shepherd. Then I went to the army and helped guard a jail in a city called Cirulnik. There was an underground military factory there. I served there from 1951 to 1954. Stalin died in 1953, while I was in the army. We cried and we thought there might be a war after his death. After the army, I came back home and worked in the militia. Later, I served as a brigadier on the collective farm.

My family is respected in our neighborhood now. If you respect yourself, everyone will respect you in return. Now, all the people come to me when they want to organize funerals or marriages or other social gatherings. Russian or Kyrgyz, it doesn't matter — all of them respect me. There is a group of elders like me and they have trusted me with leadership. Materially, we are satisfied. We have a car, a house, livestock. But that is not our wealth. Our wealth is our children.

Mrs. Kashymkan Kachikeeva

I was born in the village of Jeti Oguz in 1932. My mother died in 1933. Our father brought us up — there were six of us. Later, two joined the army, so there were four left.

I was nine when the war broke out. The actual war did not happen here, but we had hard times during the war, anyway. We saw the war in the movies, but it did not happen here. We had famine and scarcity, though. We ate spoiled potatoes. The barley crop was harvested in the spring. We would gather the leftovers grains of barley one by one, like crows. Then from those gathered grains, we would make *talkan*. We lived fine until 1942, but the cruel times began in 1943 and lasted until 1946, because everything was going to the front line.

The two leaders [Hitler and Stalin] could not get along so they fought. But Germans are the same people as we are. They wanted to occupy Moscow; we did not want to let that happen. That is all. They also wanted to get rid of Kyrgyz-*myrgyz*,[35] so they could live alone in this world. And we did not want that, of course. That is why they fought and we won. Our girls are get-

---

[35] This is a kind of nonsense term. In English, a person might say "Kyrgyz-*shmyrgyz*."

ting married to them [Germans] now. So what? We are at peace with the Germans now. Like it or not, all that has passed now. Two leaders fought and that's all there is to say about that.

In 1945, after the victory, we needed to rebuild everything that had been destroyed. We had hard lives. I think I saw nothing good during my life. I got into the local college here and studied there for two months, but then the weather got worse and I had no shoes. I was barefoot. So I had to stop going to study. I wanted an education, though.

Now, though, we have a normal life. I was 17 when I met my husband and he was 19. His family came to the village and we met each other and got married. We did not have a wedding or *kalym* [bride price] then. We just signed a certificate and that was it. Now people have the resources to pay for weddings and *kalym*s and all that. When we marry him [indicating her grandson], we will have a wedding. We did not have weddings back in our time. I had our first daughter when I was 20. Over time, I had eight children, but two of them died — one at six months and the other in her 40s — so six remain: four boys and two girls.

We had good times during Khrushchev's rule. He allowed us to keep livestock, whereas, during the war, everything was sent to the front. The 1960s were better times. There were hard, bad times before then.

During the Soviet period, the government said that there was no God. They taught us in history classes that there was no God. During funerals, they said there was no God. If you believed, they sentenced you to jail. But, of course, I believed in God. Muslims believed the whole time. Muslims are Muslim and our people are Muslim. They believed in God all the time. And now the government encourages you to believe, saying "Please support us, God!" Before, to get accepted to the party you had to deny the existence of God. Now, to be part of the party, you ask God for support. Now everyone goes to the mosques freely.

I'm not sure if we had religious schools before the war. During the war, though, there were *moldo*s [mullahs]. They were in the communities all the time, but there were no special schools for them. The young men went to the war when they were 15 or 16 and the girls worked hard in the fields. So there was no time to study. But, after the war, by the 1960s, people started learning, little by little. Before, no one would pay attention to the mosques, but later, people started to go inside the mosques.

We had opium plantations here.[36] We planted opium, raised it, and harvested it. The fields were government-controlled. We turned in the harvest and, based on the amount we had gathered, we were paid. In the 1960s and 1970s, the opium plantations were destroyed and the fields were used for other crops. When people worked in the opium fields, no one was sick; now we don't have the opium fields and everyone is sick. Then we didn't have cancer and now people die because of it. We didn't use the opium, but the process of raising it, the smell in the air, affected us.

There was no TV when I was young. We've only had TV for the past 30 years. We didn't gather with our friends to sing or dance or anything, either. How could we dance or sing when we were living in poverty and going barefoot and we had to build our households? Once I went to my friend's wedding. I spent three days there. When I returned, my mother-in-law beat me with a stick because I had left my six-month-old child home alone and the baby had gotten sick. So, one time dancing and singing was enough for my entire life. Now I can sing and dance, because my children are grown up. But if you have children, you'd better take care of them.

---

[36] According to Jenishbek Nazaraliev's 2003 book *Fatal Red Poppies*, (Medical Press: Moscow), opium poppies were officially grown in Kyrgyzstan during World War II as a way to get morphine for military hospitals. After the war, cultivation continued until 1974. The Kyrgyz used to produce 16 percent of the world's opium.

I started out working on the collective farm as a regular worker. And then I worked in the wine factory as a regular worker for 20 years. We also worked in our yard. We planted potatoes, carrots, salad, tomatoes, cucumbers, and cabbage. We worked on the land all our lives. It would have been impossible to survive otherwise. In addition to vegetables, we grew fruits like peaches, grapes, and apples. Our wages alone were not enough to support a big family like mine. Now we even use tractors on our own land, in our backyard.

My oldest daughter is married. She has 14 kids. So I consider myself happy. My great-grandson is 11 or 12. Why am I a happy person? I have children, grandchildren, and great-grandchildren and I live well and therefore I am happy. I don't live a rich life or a poor life — I have a normal lifestyle. I don't want to live a rich life, because people get scared about their money when they live rich lives. We don't even have a lock on our house, because we don't have many valuable things anyway.

25. THE ENGINEER

Joldosh Oskonbaev, who is Kyrgyz, was born in 1936. He grew up in the village of Ortosas, in Naryn oblast [province]. He graduated from a university in Bishkek and spent much of his life working at the government garage in Naryn. "The cinemas were full of Russian movies in the beginning. But then, starting in the 1960s, Kyrgyz films started to appear, too. There were big lines for the Kyrgyz movies," he recalled. Dovlet Hojamuradov and Gulzara Hayytmuradova interviewed him in Bishkek on March 21, 2009.

I had a very hard life. I have been through cold and hunger. I was in the first grade and, after nine months, the war [World War II] ended. We lived badly, because those were hard times. Starting in first grade, after classes, we helped in the fields. Everyone, including the women, harvested the grain by hand. There was always a little bit of grain left in the field and we gathered the leftovers. In Kyrgyz, we called the leftovers *mashak*.

We were given the assignment in school to gather a certain quantity of leftover grain every day. So we gathered it and brought it to the storehouse, where the deputy head of the storehouse accepted it. Then he checked to make sure we had fulfilled our assignments. If you did not gather the assigned quantity, you were punished. The punishment could include being expelled from class and school was important to us then so that was bad.

We lived in a two-room house instead of a *yurt*. We had a furnace to get us through the winter. We stoked the furnace with pressed animal dung and firewood. During the famine, we forgot how certain foods tasted. All of us just ate *talkan* [ground grain]. Sometimes we had bread. I guess, a person can get use to anything.

I had an elder brother. I also had three sisters: one was born in 1930 and another in 1932. I was born in 1936. Then there was a brother who was born in 1940 and died in 1942. My father died in 1944. He had been a shepherd. He was only 54 when he passed away. The rest of us were left with only our mother.

During the war we hated the Germans, because there was news on the radio and in the newspapers telling us about the devastating events of the war. I think the whole population hated them during the war. When we were children, our elders would even scare us by saying, "The Germans are coming!" But I was in East Germany back in 1966 and I found that Germans were very nice people. Later, I went to West Germany, too. I was invited by my relatives, who had stayed in West Germany after the war. So I took my brothers and went to visit my relatives in and I found out that West Germans were fine people, too. I think, even during the war, there were people who were fascists and people who were not.

When I was little, I liked reading the old Kyrgyz legends. I read them in Kyrgyz: Kurmanbek, Jangysh-Bayysh, Erta Byldy, Ertushik, and also, later, books by Chingis Aitmatov. I didn't read classics or Russian writers. The books were all written in the Latin alphabet back then. I don't know how, but I knew how to read that alphabet. I had an uncle who made us read every evening, especially during the winter. I think I read a couple of those books two or three times.

During my childhood, I also read newspapers. In 1944, I was in the first grade and the war ended. During the war, though, there were lots of articles about the war. Those articles were in Kyrgyz and they told us everything: about the Germans, about the events in the war zone, about the Soviet army's advances, and so on.

We liked Stalin very much back then. Everyone, adults and young people alike, sympathized with Stalin. Our teachers used to tell us that Stalin was winning the war, Stalin was feeding us, Stalin was clothing us. People could not not like him, given the circumstances.

There were five children and our mother in our family. She was busy feeding, clothing and taking care of all of us. It was hard. Then, when my older brother became a bookkeeper, our life straightened out a little bit. He was taken into the army after two years, though. There was an earthquake in Ashgabat [Turkmenistan] in 1948[37] and he served for a year there [rebuilding the city] and then he was transferred to Vladivostok and spent the rest of his service there.

I worked on the farm until fourth grade — 1948. After that, I was put to work transporting grain. The means of transportation was called a *shine* (in Kyrgyz). It was a sledge pulled by a horse. We loaded the grain onto the sledge, which looked kind of like a pair of skis. The grain was carried to one place and the hay, to another. There was no building, only a place surrounded by a fence. I did that until the seventh grade. Our school only had seven grades.

I helped on the collective farm during my free time and my vacations until the end of the seventh grade. We mostly sowed wheat and barley. The hay from them was used to feed the livestock. We also planted crops in our yard at home. Few people planted fruit in Naryn *oblast* [province], because it is one of the coldest places in Kyrgyzstan. There was no shortage of

---

[37] In 1948, Ashgabat, the capital of Turkmenistan, was hit by an earthquake that measured 7.3 on the Richter scale, which destroyed the city. Accounts of the death toll range from 10,000 to 176,000. Work crews from other parts of the Soviet Union were brought in to help rebuild the city.

fruits, though. Dungan people brought them and sold them at the local bazaars. They were lots of them during the wartime and afterwards, but later — during the 1990s — most of them left Naryn.

In 1951, I finished the seventh grade. We had two schools in the city of Naryn. Our village was five kilometers from the city. We had no watches then, so we couldn't keep time very accurately. There were times when there was a full moon in the early morning and we thought it was the sun coming up and started walking to school. When we got to school, we realized that it was too early for classes, that the school wasn't going to open for another hour or so. After school, we returned on foot, too. I did that for three years.

The village school had seven grades. It was built in 1933 and it was very cozy. Then I studied in Naryn, which was a standard school. There were two schools there: the Russian school, named after Chikalova; and the Kyrgyz school, named after Toktogul. I studied at the Toktogul school and graduated in 1954. Boys and girls studied together.

Stalin died on March 5, 1953. I was in the ninth grade in Naryn. On March 5, if I recall correctly, close to 2 p.m., he passed away. The news was broadcast on the radio. All the children, all the teachers — everyone — cried. It was a hard time when he passed away.

During my school years, groups of actors and singers from Bishkek would visit our village and perform in the local theatre. They would come once or twice a year. Their performances were in Kyrgyz and we enjoyed them. We also had a school choir. They performed from time to time, mostly during holidays. The rest of the time it was very quiet in the village.

After graduating from school, I started working on the collective farm. I could not get into university right after school because Russian was hard for me and I failed the Russian exams. The schools were fine, but we had no Russian teachers that could teach us effectively. The only Russians in the city were the military people. Well, the teachers tried to teach us, but we failed, I guess. There was a old woman teacher who cried because we were such bad students.

We had no tea back then. We had boiled water and *talkan* [ground grain]. *Talkan* is prepared by frying barley [or another type of grain] and then crushing it. So we put one spoonful of *talkan* into a glass of boiled water and that made our meal. We had this three times a day. Sometimes, at work, we had milk for lunch. It was skimmed milk — without the fat — and each person received a ration of half a liter each working day. Even after the war, in 1948, we still lived on this diet. We had this kind of hard life until the 1950s.

Back then, religion was prohibited. People believed in God anyway, though. There were one or two *moldos* [mullahs] in each village. *Moldos* read prayers during funerals or on Kurman Ait [Eid al-Adha], Orozo Ait [Ramadan], or other holidays. There were no mosques though. The *moldo*s were just invited to various places when they were needed. A *moldo* is the same as any other believer, except that he should know more about Muslim law and about the Koran. But back then, there was no difference. For instance, in our village, the *moldo*s were older people who learned Islam on their own. The youngest of the moldos was in his 40s.

There was a guy who worked as a tractor driver at the garage where I worked and he became a *moldo*. He learned about Islam on his own. No one expected him to become a religious person, because he liked to drink vodka and do other things that are not allowed in Islam. People say that he quit those kinds of things, though. All over Central Asia, there are people who like religion and learn about it on there own.

After a while, tractors started to appear and then combines. The first combines appeared in the 1960s. They were called

Stanets and they were pulled by tractors. Before that, we prepared the fields with a horse and plow and harvested the grain by hand. It was such a pain to do everything manually. Life was hard then. But people didn't object, because it was wartime. So everything was sent to the war zones. Even sheep were milked and that milk was used to make cheese and the cheese was sent to war zones. All this food belonged to the collective farm and people couldn't steal the goods that belonged to the collective farm. If a person was caught stealing, he was sent to jail. So we lived a hungry life and we had nothing to wear.

I studied at the Polytechnic Institute in Bishkek. I was accepted in 1957 and graduated in 1963. I had not been able to get in for two years after high school, because of my Russian exams. Then I went to the army in 1955 and served in a construction battalion. There were 28 people in our group from Kyrgyzstan, including Chechens, Karachays, and Ingush. We helped build factories in the Urals. There were job cuts after a year, so the army released us in 1956. My Russian improved during my service. I got back home in October of 1956 and, by 1957, I had been accepted to the Polytechnic Institute. I studied in Russian there. It was hard in the beginning, but it got easier by the third year. By then, I knew Russian pretty well. But I forgot it after graduation, since I worked in Naryn, among Kyrgyz people for 34 years and everything was in Kyrgyz.

While I was a university student, we used to go the drama theatre [in Bishkek] almost weekly. We had no discos or night clubs then, so we spent time at the cinemas. The cinemas were full of Russian movies in the beginning. But then, starting in the 1960s, Kyrgyz films started to appear, too. There were big lines for the Kyrgyz movies. We had only one dance place, which was in Dubovy Park, and it had a band. They played Russian music and waltzes and tangos. So we would go there from time to time. I didn't like dancing very much, so I rarely went there. But when I went, I used to dance the tango.

After graduation, I worked at automobile bases [government garages], as an engineer and, later, as the director of the automobile base in the city of Naryn. I was the head of the Regional Transportation Union for about 10 years. I also worked as director of the automobile [driving] school. My countrymen in my village turned to me when the reforms started and I worked there as head of the village government for four years. So, that was my career.

I got married in 1963, after I graduated from the institute. My wife was in her second year in the Medical Institute when we met in 1962. She is from the Issyk-Kul *oblast* [province] and I am from Naryn *oblast* [province], so two people from neighboring regions got married.

Khrushchev came to power after Stalin. There was a meeting in Moscow and he presented himself in that meeting, praising himself, saying that there would be enough grain for three to five years. The year after his speech, 1963, there was a famine all over the Soviet Union. There was bread, but not enough. Everyone stood in long lines to get bread. I was working in the city of Jalal-Abad back then. I remember standing in a long line, starting early in the morning, to get some bread. Khrushchev had lied to the people. He was not the best leader; he was just a braggart. Well, he was replaced in 1963.

Khrushchev's successor was Brezhnev. People started to live better during Brezhnev's time. People started to buy cars. In comparison to the Khrushchev era, the living standard increased. The reason is probably that he was a good leader and a good manager. He made our lives better.

In 1963, my family was in Jalal-Abad with me. I was working as a mechanical engineer in the local automobile base there. My wife was working as a nurse in the Jalal-Abad hospital. We were just recent university graduates, so we only got a two-room apartment. Our salaries were good, though. I earned 80 *ruble*s and so did she. That was more than enough for us and the kids. We could cover food, clothing, and expenses.

The minister of our republic [the Kyrgyz Soviet Socialist Republic] visited us in Jalal-Abad in 1964. So I signed up for the meeting and showed up. At the meeting, he asked me why I'd come and I told him I wanted to be transferred home to my region, Naryn. He told me to go and work in Naryn and signed the order for my transfer. Ever since then, I have stayed in Naryn and lived well. In Naryn, the government gave us an apartment and we lived there with our children until 1976. Then I built a house and we lived there.

Until the 1970s, we used to dry fruits and vegetables. However, starting in the 1970s, the technology of canning was popularized and soon it became part of the everyday lives of our people. People started to can jams and salads.

In the 1980s, Gorbachev came to power. He was a member of the Politburo, so we knew who he was. First he became the secretary of the TsK [Central Committee of the Communist Party].Then he got to the top and started his *perestroika*. I think it did not work out. For example, he wanted to prohibit vodka. Russian people didn't like that, so they started to make vodka on their own. Even Kyrgyz people started doing it. Kyrgyz people didn't even know what vodka was before the Russians came. The Russians brought vodka to Kyrgyzstan. I think people in Issyk-Kul province started drinking it first and then the people of Naryn caught on and left them behind.

My wife and I have five children now: two boys and five girls. We had one more boy, but he was a brat; one day he fell from the roof and died. He was a good student, but misbehaved himself from time to time. Now we have only two sons. All of my children have higher educations. My oldest son graduated from Lomonosov Moscow State University. My oldest daughter is a doctor. My second daughter graduated with a degree in economics. My youngest daughter graduated from Bishkek Humanitarian University. My youngest son got accepted to Slavic University, stopped his studies, and left for England. After he returned home, he graduated from that university with a degree in economics.

We moved to Bishkek in 1997. My eldest son brought us here a year after I start losing my sight. The local doctors operated on me, but they did it wrong. Then, in 2003, my youngest son took me to Germany for another operation. After that, I could see well — more or less. Then, in 2007, my grandson got sick and he used to cry a lot. On July 13, I got stressed out because of all the noise in the house — all the crying — and the next day I couldn't see.

26. The Factory Worker

Dilber Ejeke,[38] who is half Tatar and half Uzbek, was born in 1941 in Tashkent, Uzbekistan. After graduating from a university there, she moved to Kyrgyzstan, to live with relatives. "The Crimean Tatars were ... the first ones who brought the technique of canning to our area. They introduced the greenhouse to local agriculture. The first cucumbers and tomatoes were also harvested by Crimean Tatars," she recalled. Dovlet Hojamuradov and Gulzara Hayytmuradova interviewed her in Bishkek on March 9, 2009.

We lived with my mother. I lost my dad in the war and my mother did not marry again. She was busy with her job so I would come home and just take care of myself. Sometimes she would be on the night shift. So waiting for her so that we could eat together did not make sense. I guess I matured early. I could take care of myself from an early age. In the second or third grade, I could already cook.

The war was devastating. The war zones like Ukraine, Belarus, and parts of Russia were destroyed. I know about this from the media and from my own experiences in Minsk [the capital of Belarus] and other places, after the war. There were some proposals to rebuild Minsk in another place. But the people wanted to rebuild it in its old location and that's what happened.

---

[38] She declined to give her family name, citing privacy concerns. So she asked to be called "Dilber *Ejeke*." *Eje* is a Kyrgyz term of respect for older woman. *Ejeke* is the diminutive form.

It was a hard time — not only for those people in the European part of the USSR, but for everyone. We were all in one state. Since we had fewer men after the war, we — the women — played a big role in the reconstruction. There were lots of female workers in the factories and in the fields. My husband was raised in a rural area, unlike me — I was brought up in the city. So he was used to seeing women doing hard jobs, like carrying heavy things. Thus, he believed that women could do all kinds of jobs. Once, he told me to go get a heavy sack. I was shocked and looked at him with a confused look. He gave me a confused look right back. I thought about the period he grew up in and then I understood his confusion and his expectations. He was born in 1938 and, by 1943, he was five years old. He was raised in a social environment where every woman did hard work.

We worked our land, we raised potatoes in our backyard. They are, as you know, known as "the second bread." We also raised fruit and vegetables like tomatoes, cucumbers, lettuce, and cabbage. Our vegetable field was not very big. The majority of the arable land belonged to the collective farm and was used to grow grain.

We dried almost everything to preserve it. This was an especially good way to save fruits for the winter. Crimean Tatars were deported to Uzbekistan during the war.[39] We never had Bulgarian peppers [sweet, light-green peppers] before they arrived. They were the ones who added Bulgarian peppers to Central Asian cuisine. Thanks to them, we have traditional dishes like *goluptsy* — Bulgarian peppers stuffed with rice and meat, in broth.

The Crimean Tatars were also the first ones who brought the technique of canning to our area. They introduced the

---

[39] On 18-20 May 1944, Stalin had the Crimean Tatars deported from Crimea, on Ukraine's Black Sea coast, to Uzbekistan and other parts of the Soviet Union.

greenhouse to local agriculture. The first cucumbers and tomatoes were also harvested by Crimean Tatars. In the 1950s, my friend and I were invited to Piskend, the region in Uzbekistan where all the Crimean Tatars lived. We were invited to the house of my friend's brother, who was married to a Tatar woman. She said that her sister-in-law could cook Bulgarian peppers and could also can them. So we went to see how she did it.

We arrived after a long bus trip. My friend's brother's Tatar wife prepared those famous peppers in a delicious sauce and served them in a huge bowl. After we were done eating, she took me to watch the canning process. They took champagne bottles and filled them with tomato juice. Then she closed the opening with sealing wax. Later, in 1960, mass canning started. Everyone was canning with the special jars and lids that we use now. *Muraba* [jams] had been in Central Asia for a long time already, but the techniques and materials for canning them only arrived in the 1960s. Before that, they were always saved in cool places, but then people started living in apartments and things changed and one way of preserving fruits and other things was canning.

Kyrgyzstan was always good for growing fruits. Almost all regions of the country can produce fruits. Therefore, there is no scarcity of fruits to can for the winter. Furthermore, it's possible to can fruits for future winters. For example, we still have canned jams from a year ago.

My grandmother lived in a rural area and, in the summertime, my mother would take me there while she helped my grandmother with her work on the collective farm. My parents worked in the collective farm fields and they would take me there because there were few kindergartens, especially in the rural areas. So I would be in the field with them while they were harvesting. They made me a small bag to play with. Well, I played with it in the field where the grain was gathered. I filled the bag and then emptied it, filled it and emptied it. This cycle of self-entertainment lasted all day. At the end of the day, I hid the little bag of grain inside my shirt and carried it home.

Taking grain was a serious offence and could lead to a cruel punishment, like being sentenced to jail. So everyone was checked — except for the kids. So that's how I gathered a half a bucket of grain in one season. I was three or four years old, so I know this about myself from stories my parents told. One of the other stories about my childhood is that I got so used to going to the fields and playing with the grain that when I lost that little bag, I panicked and cried.

In the post-war period, there were few men. I remember, in the 1950s, when my mother and her friends would gather, there were no men at all. If there were one or two, then they had definitely been wounded in the war. After the war, the men that survived were very nervous. The local *pivnushki* [pubs] were where men gathered and drank. When they got drunk, they would always fight and make a lot of noise. Nowadays, people drink but, unless they're youngsters, they don't fight. But, back then, the pubs were associated with fighting. I realized later that the men were nervous and that those fights were "post-war wars." Since they were wounded — they had lost hands, legs, and other parts of their bodies — it was a difficult, depressing time for them.

The women worked. The ones who lost their men got a certain amount of money from the government. I went to school and my mother worked and earned money We were not living in luxury but we were not hungry. I studied at Russian School No. 65 in Tashkent. The school had two shifts: the first-shift classes started in the morning; the second-shift classes started in the afternoon. All the elementary school children studied in the first shift.

Well, my academic years started in 1949-1950. There were separate male and female schools for younger students at that time. However, in the seventh grade, the male and female classes merged. Half of our school was transferred to the boys' school and half of the boys' school was transferred to the girls' school. This change was problematic at first, since the boys and girls were embarrassed and avoided one another. As time went by, though, the division disappeared.

My first language is Russian. I went to a Russian kindergarten, a Russian school, and a Russian institute. I also worked in a Russian environment. Kyrgyz people are nomadic, so they didn't create cities. Bishkek was founded 140 years ago by Russians. Therefore, there was only a small indigenous population in the city. However, [Kyrgyz] young people would come to the city to study and they would stay in the city and become russified. Shepherds' children would come and study and live here. This began the process of russification of the whole population.

Although my first language is Russian, I also know the Turkic languages. I understand Turkmen, I know Kyrgyz and Uzbek and Kazakh. I never learned them on purpose — I just began to understand them through social interactions throughout my life. Foreign languages were taught in the schools. For instance, I learned French in school. There was English at the institute and everyone who studied a language other than English in high school was taught basic English.

In school everything was in Russian during class but, the rest of the time, everyone talked freely in his or her own language. It was a normal thing and no one was embarrassed about it. It was natural. At work, it was the same. There was no requirement that you had to know Russian, but everyone knew it because of the educational system. I would talk to Russian people in Russian and to local people in their own languages. I guess I didn't even think about it; it just happened so naturally.

We got used to each others' languages and cultures during our university years. When we saw each other, we would greet each other in our own languages. For example, when we were building our dormitory one summer, I was exposed to Azeri culture. Now, when I see my Azeri neighbors, I greet them in their own language.

There were diasporas of different nationalities in my university. They would gather together and hold on to each other. I guess blood binds people and their place of birth did matter after all, once they were outside of their motherlands. I could never take part in their parties and, thus, I was never fully introduced to any of their cultural traditions except language.

All sorts of people came to Kyrgyzstan. I know Volga Germans,[40] for example, who were sent to Kyrgyzstan, and Crimean Tatars, and people from the Caucasus and from Uzbekistan. I didn't know any Karachays, Chechens, or Kabardins,[41] but I later found out that they had been resettled to Kyrgyzstan. There were also Adyghes[42] in Uzbekistan. When I moved here and started working, I found out more about the nationalities that had been resettled in Kyrgyzstan. There were also Koreans[43] and Jews in Uzbekistan.

---

[40] On 3-20 September 1941, Stalin had the Volga Germans deported from Russia's Volga region to Kazakhstan, Siberia, and other parts of the Soviet Union, fearing they might collaborate with Germany during the war.

[41] Stalin had the Karachay deported from the Caucasus on 2 November 1943. He had some Kabardins deported from the Caucasus to Central Asia and other parts of the Soviet Union in 1944. That same year, Stalin had all the Chechens deported from Chechnya to Siberia and Central Asia.

[42] Adyghes, also known as Circassians, are from the Republic of Adygea, in Russia, in the northwest Caucasus.

[43] See "The Deportee," Sofiya Kim's oral history, pp112-115 in this volume.

And there were lots of people who had been evacuated from the war zones [during World War II]. For instance, Dora Pavlovna had been evacuated from the war zone and told to live with my aunt. The authorities said she would live with them and so she did. There was another elderly couple that had no place to stay and was ordered to stay with us. My mom said that they had been on the road for so long that they were dirty and covered with bugs.

There were no conflicts among all these different types of people; everyone was tolerant. I guess trouble brings people together. Lots of the people who moved here back then, stayed here. For instance, Dora Pavlovna stayed. But the Jews migrated to Israel after *perestroika*. Lots of Jews I knew from work left to Israel, like Yashka Sigalton, and others.

I remember when Stalin died, someone put the radio in the hallway. Even before he actually died, his condition had been broadcast. Everyone was crying and in a bad mood in those days. It was such a tragedy. I cried, too. There were funerals all over. I remember that, in the square in Tashkent, there was a huge memorial in his honor and I remember, at one event, there were artificial flowers, but on the day of his death, the elders prepared a special wreath of violets for him. Back then, there weren't as many real flowers as there are now. I was 12 in 1953 and was amazed to see that wreath. The violets were so beautiful and they were surrounded with big green leaves.

When I was in school, from time to time, we were taken to the Youth Theatre, the Opera House, and concerts — especially Children's Concerts — and to exhibitions of children's crafts. I liked needlework. It was poplar then to do needlework with simple crosses and Bulgarian crosses. In the theaters, there were interesting shows in Russian and Uzbek. The concerts would be performances by artists from all over the USSR. On our own, we would go to the cinema. We enjoyed these things mostly during our student years.

The first-shift classes started with physical exercises every day. We were not allowed into the school until we did our exercises, so we did light exercises every day and then we would go inside and study.

Since we were from the post-war generation, there were lots of students from the orphanage. The kids who lost parents during the war were evacuated to Central Asia. There were lots of orphanages built. They stayed there, but studied with us in the schools. We didn't realize that they were orphans because they dressed the same as us. There was no indication that they were hungry or anything. For example, the kids from the orphanage would bring cookies and offer them to us, but they would never take any cookies from other kids, because they were too proud. Our efforts to share with them were always rebuffed.

Our school was very international.However, there weren't ethnic divisions. Besides, those times were so harsh and controlled that there was no chance for things like that. There were Russians, Tatars, Uzbeks, Kyrgyz, and Jews. Lots of languages were used around us. We also studied a foreign language after the fourth grade — it was French in our school.

There were no clubs in our school. However, if there were any students who were not good at their lessons, the teachers would work with them outside class. Students from the first shift would stay after their classes. Students from the second shift would come the next morning to catch up.

There was a Dvorets Pionerov [Palace of Pioneers[44]] in every region and every city. There were lots of clubs there, including dancing, drawing, sewing, and music clubs. I went to a dancing club, which affected my life later. I liked to waltz best. There was a piano in the hallway and I don't know why, but our French teacher would play waltzes every day and we

---

[44] The Young Pioneers was a Soviet youth organization similar to the Boy/Girl Scouts in the U.S.

danced. Maybe that was the reason why I liked dancing and, especially, the waltz.

We did not avoid boys then, but the boys mostly wouldn't dance. So girls paired up with each other and danced. We had graduation balls as well. We would order special dresses and walk in the parks. For girls, special dresses were part of the ball. Back then, it was less common for factories to make special dresses, so we found private seamstresses to make them for us.

After the seventh grade, we were taken to pick cotton. I think it was like that all over the USSR. The city students were taken to work on the collective farms after the seventh grade, but the rural kids started collecting cotton even earlier. The city students would be taken to the rural areas on a big bus. During the harvest, we lived near where we worked. We took sheets to sleep on and would live in the schools out there, which were closed for the harvest. We got our food from the collective farms. We didn't have any classes, we just worked during the day and had fun in the evening.  Locals would present different games and performances for us every day. We liked it, since we had no school, no quotas, and good weather, since the work started on September 20. But they didn't pay us — I guess they spent the money for our food, instead.

While I was studying at the institute, too, they would take us to pick cotton to help fulfill the government plan starting September 20 — but then they would pay us. It wasn't very much money, but it was enough for students. The collective farm fed us well. They would bring the food to the fields. It was mainly lunch. Breakfast and dinner were provided in the rural schools where we stayed.

The Kyrgyz students were taken to the farms to work, too. For example, the students from the Medical Academy were taken to Osh *oblast* [province] to collect cotton; the students from the Polytechnic University were taken to the Kemin Valley to collect potatoes; and other students from the Medical Academy were to Talas *oblast* [province] to pick tobacco. I know this because my peers told me about it after I moved to Kyrgyzstan. One student who went to the Kemin Valley had an allergic reaction to the tobacco leaves. Picking cotton was not so bad. The weather would be cool and we would pick until October or, sometimes, November.

My father was an educated person, so my mother was always telling me to study hard and apply to the institute. She always told me about the advantages of education and advised me to study and read a lot. So I read lots of literature, especially about the war. Also, I read western literature like [Theodor] Dreiser, [Guy de] Maupassant, Jack London and, of course, [Alexander] Pushkin and [Mikhail] Lermontov.

We were raised on patriotic literature. I read *Povest o Zoye i Shure*,[45] *Molodaya Gvardiya*,[46] and *Chetvertaya Vysota*[47] (about

---

[45] "The Story of Zoya and Shura," (1978), by Lyubov Kosmodemiyanskaya is about the author's daughter and son — Zoya and Alexander (in Russian, "Shura" is a nickname for Alexander) — who were legendary Soviet heroes of World War II. Zoya, born in 1923, fought as a partisan against the Germans. She was caught and tortured, but refused to give information about her comrades. Then she was hanged.

[46] The Young Guard," (1946), by Alexander Fadeyev, is a novel based on real events of World War II, about an underground anti-fascist youth organization, the Young Guard, which resisted the Nazis occupation of Krasnodon, Ukraine.

[47] "Fourth Height," (1946), by Elena Ilina, is about Gulia Korolyova, a hero of World War II. It tells about her childhood, her school years and about her death on the front.

Gulya). They affected me so much that I would cry while I was reading them. Once, my mom came home from her job and found me crying. When she asked why I was crying, I told her I was crying about Zoya, the hero from the book I was reading, who had been hanged.

In the summer, we would gather in Uzbekistan and make salads from cucumbers and tomatoes. We ate fruits like melons, watermelons, peaches, and grapes. During the day, we would eat fruits and, in the evenings, we would have something hot for dinner. Bread and fruit — like grapes or watermelons — were my favorite meal in the summertime. I still have the habit of eating watermelon or grapes with bread. These days we usually eat fruit after the meal, as desert. But I still eat it with bread, even if I am full.

Dating was different when I was young. Boys took us to the cinema and treated us to ice cream and soda. Later, when my son grew up and started dating and asked me for money, I told him, playing the part of a mother who is trying to be economical with the family budget: "Buy her an ice cream and let her lick it once and then you can lick it once and you can both be happy." He laughed, knowing I was joking. Dates in our time consisted of walking in the park, and that's why the Russian word *gulyat* [to go for a walk] has the connotation of dating. The only time my husband and I went to a restaurant was after we registered our marriage at Zaks [the state marriage registration office]. There was a restaurant near the World War II memorial called Druzhba [Friendship] and he took me there.

When I was younger, we would go to the cinema. There wereno TVs until the end of the 1950's. The first TVs were small and you placed them behind big lenses filled with some kind of liquid. The lens would enlarge the picture. My first movie was Mat [Mother], based on a work by [Maxim] Gorky. At the cinemas, there were lines everywhere: for getting a ticket, for getting into the cinema. It wasn't easy to get in.

People would also roam in the parks in the evenings. Nowadays, people don't understand parks, but our generation was different. Our parents would take us to the parks for ice cream, soda, and dances. There was always live music in the parks. The elders would dance and the kids would run and play. They had different kinds of music, like folk music and waltzes.

The parks were beautiful. Bishkek's Panfilov Park, especially, was so green and full of flowers and it always had music. The Ala-Too Cinema was part of Dubovy Park back then. There were two cinemas back then — Udarnik and Ala-Too. There were also ice cream vendors and flowers in the park in the 1950s. Erkindik Street was Djerjinski Street back then and it was a place for gathering. It was very beautiful — there were lights that looked like bells and they were so bright.

In the post-war period, there were often gatherings in the evening. In the cities, especially, the lights made it as bright as daytime. My husband once told me he had been surprised to come from his village to the city and find that, at night, it was as bright as daytime. There were fountains everywhere. Panfilov and Dubovy parks had fountains and, near the Udarnik cinema there was another fountain.

There were parades on November 7,[48] May 1,[49] and May 9,[50] with grand marches and bands playing. Each organization presented its products and had its own band. They would all carry slogans like "Forward to the victory of communism," "Way to go — CPSS [Communist Party of the Soviet Union]," "We will give our country a certain amount of coal or a certain

---

[48] The anniversary of the October Revolution of 1917. It is in November because, until the revolution, Russia still used the Julian calendar, rather then the Gregorian.

[49] Labor Day.

[50] Victory Day, the anniversary of the end of World War II, known as "The Great Patriotic War" in Russian.

amount of cotton," etc. That's how we lived under socialism. Everyone presented their products on moving vehicles that were colorful and beautiful. Everyone was dancing and singing — it was fun. Victory Day was a triumphant celebration of our veterans. November 7 was the day when the country's military might was put on display, followed by civilian organizations, and sportsmen with their performances.

It was hard to get into a university through the formal procedure, but I would not know about any informal procedures, because I got accepted in the regular way, by passing the exams. But there were people who could not get in. For example, my friend was short by one point on the entrance exam, so she became a "reservist." Well, the first semester at the institute was harsh and there were no second chances.

Once you got disqualified, a reservist would take your place. So she was lucky and got in in this way, without getting the required score on the test.

Cheating always existed. People cheated on essay exams, especially. We would make cheat sheets — folded pieces of paper — and hide them underneath our watches so that no one would find them. Not everyone was given the essay writing test, though. There were exams in math, chemistry, and essay writing. I applied to the Department of Chemical Technologies at the Tashkent Textile Institute.

You could get a regular stipend or a high stipend. The high stipends were for excellent students. The regular ones were 35 *rubles*. That was enough back then, since bread cost 10 or 12 *kopeks* and *piroshki* [savory pastries stuffed with meat, cabbage, potatoes or other fillings] cost 3 *kopeks* each. Students with families would go to the train station to earn a little extra money by loading and unloading goods — the men, that is.

We did not have international exchange students at that time. Students could move around within the borders of the

USSR, but not beyond. As we were finishing the institute, though, a group went to Czechoslovakia, which was a socialist state at the time. It was such a sensation, but it only happened as we were leaving. Leaving the Soviet Union was unusual when I was young. It wasn't until the 1970s that people began to go outside the Union's borders to travel and work. Then they would go to socialist states like Finland, Bulgaria, East Germany, Hungary, or Czechoslovakia, but certain documents from the regional committee were required. So people preferred to vacation within the borders of the USSR, for example in the Baltic states. I visited all three Baltic states: Lithuania, Latvia, and Estonia.

You could go anywhere and work, but you could only work in the specialty that was on your diploma. There were a lot of workers who came from Russia. In the Konvolno-Sukonnom Kombinat [factory], there were lots of specialists from Russia. Those specialists had graduated from universities in Moscow, Kiev, and Leningrad. This was during the period of "mass graduation" after the war and light industry was just developing, especially in Central Asia. Thus, we didn't have indigenous people who were specialists in light industry. So specialists came from Russia. They weren't only recent graduates; more experienced workers also came. They worked in administrative and key specialist positions.

Later, the local people were sent to study these specialties, too. For example, lots of Kyrgyz students studied in Tashkent to prepare for careers in light industry. Turkmen and Kazakhs did the same. In the other republics, there were no institutes offering that type of education, so Tashkent was the center for light industry specialists. These specialists learned about refining cotton and wool, and about textile technologies. Students came to Tashkent from all over Central Asia and the Caucasus. The distribution of educational opportunities was based on nationality and on the available post-graduation work opportunities.

I remember when Khrushchev was in power. It was when I was studying at the institute. He got interested in growing corn and, after that, there wasn't much wheat. I remember that people had to stand in long lines to get bread. That's what I remember about Khrushchev.

Then came the Brezhnev period. That was when I started work. As young specialists, my husband and I were given an apartment. There were lots of jobs and the salaries were good. We earned enough and the apartment was fine. First, we got a two-room apartment and, later, we moved to a three-room apartment when we had two sons. Under Brezhnev, we worked and saw the best times of socialism.

It was the best time for Kyrgyzstan's development, too. Light industry was developed during that period. We had 24 different organizations and unions working in light industry. We were providing citizens with clothing. We produced fabrics for suits and for coats, we produced silk and cotton. We produced clothing for people of all ages, from babies to elderly people.

During the Brezhnev period, maternity leave was extended to three months and a "baby boom" started. Then there was a shortage of children's socks and long pants, because we had only one factory that produced them. Over the next two years, another factory was built at the intersection of Almatinskaya and Gorkogo streets to produce these goods. Later, these goods were even exported, since they were 100 percent cotton.

We were responsible for children's clothing, so the Ministry of Health would check our factory and the goods it produced. The shoes had to be made from real leather and everything else — t-shirts, suits, and shirts — had to be made from real cotton. Now things are not the same. Now we have synthetic goods from China, which are cheap and not as healthy as cotton.

Imports from other socialist states were in abundance in Central Asia during the Soviet times. So guests from the

European part of the Union would buy a lot of those goods here: shoes from Finland and Czechoslovakia — everything was natural. We had imports from China then, too. But they were natural, not like the goods now. Everything was natural during those years. One of my wedding presents from my mother was a length of natural Chinese silk cloth. Even other goods like shoes, coats, t-shirts, and dresses were all-natural.

We could satisfy the needs of the republic [the Kyrgyz Soviet Socialist Republic] easily. We even sent goods to other republics. We produced 7 million meters per year of fabric. We had two leather factories, two shoe cooperatives, a shoe factory in Kyzyl-Kyyal, and the Frunzinskoye Shoe Cooperative. There was also the Dom Modeli [the Fashion House]. That's where new styles were created and then, from there, they were sold to the factories for mass production.

We had some professional top models. One was Mila and the other was Iteri, they were beautiful half-Georgian girls. Others were recruited, too — especially kids — for the presentation of clothing. Now fashion is very different. Our styles were very ordinary and simple compared to what people wear now.

Creativity was encouraged in our workplaces. There were special funds for creativity and anyone who offered worthy innovations was granted some of the money from these funds. We took part in presentations and competitions. There were also the competitions between the different organizations for the quality and quantity of products.

Then it was time for Gorbachev's *perestroika*. The job cuts started and so people had to start brainstorming about how to survive. Some people started doing business, going to China, Turkey, the Baltic states, and Korea and bringing back goods to sell. Others used their skills, like needlework and sewing. All these people were educated, but they were still just hauling around bags of goods. Their education was not enough for survival. Artists, PhDs, and teachers were working in the bazaars.

There was one teacher sitting by me in the market and she would always wear dark glasses, since she was embarrassed that her students might see her.

In the beginning, everyone was ashamed of doing business. But a teacher's salary was not enough to support a family. The only option was to find alternative ways to earn money. The ones who had vehicles started taxi businesses. Foreigners thought that we would die of hunger, but they didn't count on our 100 percent literacy rate. I think that our literacy helped our society survive those harsh conditions and radical changes. So that's how capitalism started here.

The changes under *perestroika* were very strange. My son broke his finger and we brought him to the hospital and the doctors said we had to pay. I was confused about what we needed to pay for. It took us some time to get used to the idea that we had to pay for everything.

As capitalism took hold, local industries lost their customers. Imported goods were of poorer quality, but people were going through a difficult period and they only cared that the imports were cheaper. Thus, the local factories that produced better quality— but relatively expensive— goods went out of business. For example, the carpet factory went bankrupt because of cheaper Chinese and Iranian imports. Other organizations faced the same competitive conditions.

Our generation saw everything from the war to the collapse of the USSR. Nevertheless I think we saw less than our parents saw before and during the war. My uncle's stories about the famine in Kazakhstan could make you cry. He told us he once caught a live frog and ate it. He used to say that famine was a devastating thing. The famine touched everyone. I remember my parents and my sister crying, remembering the harsh days that they had been through.

Now my family is fine. I have two sons living in Bishkek.

One is married, the other is still single. I have one granddaughter. I am retired. I get a pension and the government has promised to increase it in April.

27. The Kidnapped Bride

Buburakan Muratbekova, who is Kyrgyz, was born in 1936 in the village of Karakol in Kyrgyzstan's Talas oblast [province]. She was bride-kidnapped when she was 17. She worked as a librarian. "The role of women has always been to take care of the household, starting with bearing the children and ending with growing potatoes," she said. Dilbar Ruzadorova interviewed her in the village of Chat Bazaar, in Talas oblast on March 15, 2009.

I was born in small village called Karakol, in Talas *oblast* [province]. People in Karakol could only grow potatoes back then, because of the cold climate. We had no bazaars, so every household had to grow something in order to live.

I was only 5 years old when the war started. I didn't understand much of what was going on. I only remember how my mother grieved when she sent her sons — my brothers — to war. My family was very big. I had 13 siblings, seven of whom, unfortunately, I do not remember at all. The remaining seven included four brothers, one older sister, and me.

Many men were forced to leave their homes and fight in the war. This problem touched my family as well. All four of my brothers went to the war. The oldest left us when he was 19. I remember that he had moved to Bishkek to study, but, due to the war, he had to leave all that behind.

He fought in Ukraine. He used to write us letters about his victories and defeats. I still remember the excitement and the tears of happiness in my mother's eyes each time she got a letter from him. His last letter was about a battle on the Don. After that, we heard no other news from him.

My second brother was sent to the war when he was 17. When he left us, he left us forever. We never heard anything from him again. My third brother was sent first to flight school and then to the war. We received letters from him, but not for long. After all these losses, sorrow and sadness settled on our family, but our parents tried not to show their pain to us.

My fourth brother fought for two years and was wounded and sent home. When he arrived, my parents' joy and delight was immeasurable. However, after a while, when my brother got well, they [the army] called him back. My brother and 14 other people ran away to the mountains to avoid the war. After several days, they were caught and sent to Komsomolsk-on-Amur [in the Russian Far East], for 10 years. After 10 years, my brother came home healthy and started a family. He was the only one of my brothers who came back from the war.

After the war, we started to search for information about my brothers. We looked through the archives of the *voenkomat* [the military commissariat] and found out that my oldest brother was buried in Ukraine. Apparently, he had gotten married there and had a son. Later, his son tried to find us, but for some reason, my father didn't want to meet him. We also learned that my second brother had died in a train crash on his way to the war and the third one was killed in the war. Thus, I lost three of my brothers and my parents lost three of their sons.

After the war, when Stalin died, I remember that everybody was in great pain. People of all ages and genders in my village — I was living in Chat Bazar then — cried for several days. I remember I also cried, but I didn't really understand why I was crying. I just cried because everyone else was crying.

I studied in the school in Karakol until the tenth grade — back then, that was the highest grade. Classes started at 8 a.m., but we woke up a lot earlier, because we had a bunch of other things to do around the house. I liked school a lot and always prepared for my classes. We learned how to read, write, and count. Without such skills you can't make your way in this world. We studied math, literature, Kyrgyz language, and other subjects. My favorite was literature. I don't remember having any extracurricular activities. Back then we had no extra time for such activities.

We played different games, though. Back then we were not allowed to play with the boys or even to hang around with them. One of the games was called *ak-chulmuk*; in it, we threw bones and then looked for them. I also liked cooking and sewing. TV didn't arrive in our village until 1964.

Unfortunately, after graduating from school, I wasn't able to continue my education. There were several reasons and one of them was the fact that my parents were already middle-aged and I had to take care of them. There were other reasons, but my parents were the most significant.

In 1954, when I was 19, I got married to a man who stole me from my parents. I was stolen by Sovet Muratbekov and, after a while, we got married. He was three years older than me. My husband had studied in a medical school in Bishkek, but didn't graduate because of a very odd incident. During one procedure, some blood had splattered on his legs and he got sick. He was so ill that his parents decided to bring him home so they could take care of him. For a long time, he couldn't walk and it was only after massaging his legs with *jir barsuka* [badger fat] that he managed to return to normal life. After that, he didn't continue his medical studies. Instead, he transferred to the biology department. We got married when he came back from Bishkek. Then he worked as a biology teacher in the local high school.

The role of women has always been to take care of the household, starting with bearing the children and ending with growing potatoes. If, back then, women were only involved in household activities, now they work for the government and other organizations. Women have much more freedom now. They can go to mosques if they want to and no one will think it is strange. In our times, girls were not considered smart enough to go to school, but now, I'm glad to say, the situation has changed.

Men have been always been thought of as the breadwinners of the family. If, today, men work in offices and earn money, in the past, their jobs were much more physically difficult. They had to herd animals, work in the fields, and do the heavy work at home. The main thing that makes a strong and healthy family is mutual understanding and support between the husband and the wife. Also, for a perfect family, your kids should be well-educated.

I have three children: one son, Manasbek; and two daughters, Chinara and Mayramkan. All of them have their own families now. My son lives in Bishkek, my older daughter lives in Aral, and my younger daughter lives with me.

My family had a big farm in Karakol and we grew only potatoes. But, in Chat Bazar we can grow tomatoes, onions, potatoes and other kinds of vegetables. Over the years, agricultural technology changed a lot and it became much easier to keep animals and to grow everything. Of course, with better technology, people started to grow more crops and, surely, machines like combines made the work easier.

I truly supported collectivization, because, under collectivization, everything was distributed fairly. We all worked on the collective farms and received equal rewards. Moreover, the government helped us even with our domestic affairs. Privatization ruined everything. People started to buy and sell their lands, animals, and houses. It was profitable for those in power. They were powerful enough to take land away from those who weren't as powerful. Many people lost everything.

The sense of equality diminished and the attitude became "the strongest first."

We still grow our own food, just like all our neighbors. Chat Bazar is much warmer than Karakol, so we can grow almost everything here, from tomatoes, potatoes, cucumbers, and onions, to apples, cherries and more. But the most widely grown crop is potatoes. We eat them ourselves and we sell them for money to buy other things.

My favorite food has always been *beshbarmak*, which is our national food and is eaten by all Kyrgyz. I'm not very picky about my food, though. Whatever my daughter cooks for the whole family, I eat. I prefer to eat Kyrgyz food, though. And I don't drink alcohol. I have never had alcohol in my life. Our [Kyrgyz] food has not changed in my lifetime. We still cook *beshbarmak* the same way we used to. I must say that when I was younger I could eat more than I do now — that's because of my health and age, of course.

When we were young, we had no restaurants in our village. Everybody ate at home. The food was mainly made from potatoes, meat, and bread. Back then we needed "strong" food, because we worked a lot. In my old age, I have been to restaurants several times. I must say they have all kinds of food, which I have never seen before, much less eaten. But I still prefer my own *beshbarmak* at home. My granddaughter told me that now, in restaurants, you can find Chinese, Korean, Indian, and European food. In the past, we had only traditional meals in cafeterias and restaurants.

My religion is Islam. I'm a Sunni Muslim. My whole family is Muslim. There were no religious schools in Talas in the past and none of my family members ever attended a religious school. My parents fasted [on Ramadan], I remember. But I have only a very cloudy memory of me fasting. I haven't fasted in recent years, that's for sure.

We are much freer to practice our religion now than we were during the Soviet times. My parents used to pray before the Soviet Union, but then they stopped. Before the Soviet times, we had mosques, but no churches. My family never faced any difficulties because of our religion, but I know that in many cases the Soviets jailed people who prayed or took part in any kind of religious activity. I heard a story about one *moldo* [mullah], who was put in jail and wasn't even allowed to wash his face the way every Muslim does before praying and they tried to keep him from praying. However, people say his faith was so strong that every time when the time for praying arrived, the doors opened by themselves. Moreover, when one of the guards tried to stop him, he got sick and eventually died.

I started praying in my late 60s. Now my health doesn't allow me to pray. But, usually, men pray in the mosque and women pray in their houses. It was the same when I was younger. Women had to cover their heads and wear long skirts while praying, both at home and in mosques.

My first language was Kyrgyz, my parents speak Kyrgyz, and I don't know any other languages. I just speak a little bit of broken Russian. I have always spoken Kyrgyz at home and at work and everywhere else. In the village, Kyrgyz is considered the most prestigious language, because everybody knows it. I haven't been to the city for a long time. Therefore, I don't know about the situation there, but I suppose Russian is the most widely used language there.

I have never lived in the city. In the villages, people are more hardworking and are more likely to be willing to work if you ask them — that's something that cannot be said about the people in the cities. Also, children in the villages are healthier than children in the city. If I had to move to the city, I would take my animals and my handcrafts and other supplies, so I could continue my work. But I would rather stay in the village than move to the city.

My son works in the city and sends me money sometimes. Since my husband left us in 1997, my children have supported me. These days I get my pleasure from spending time with my grandchildren. I appreciate every moment of that time and will remember it forever. My grandchildren mean a lot to me.

28. The Writer

Sooronbay Jusuyev, who is Kyrgyz, was born in 1925 in the village of Kyzl-Jar. He served in World War II and then built a career as one of Kyrgyzstan's most famous writers. He has published dozens of books and has translated Shakespeare's Hamlet — among other works — into Kyrgyz. Dilbar Ruzadorova interviewed him in Bishkek on March 20, 2009.

I grew up with my mother and four sisters. We lived in Kyzyl-Jar, in the Kara-Kuljyn region of Osh oblast [province]. My parents worked on a collective farm. Nowadays, my younger sister — who lives in the village — and I, are still alive. My other three sisters have passed away.

My father was the first person in Kyzyl-Jar to bring up the idea of building a mosque, and he eventually did it. To go there, men and women had to cover their heads and women had to wear dresses. In those days, no one was put in jail for practicing Islam, but sometimes government officials were fired because of their religious views.

I am a Muslim, officially, but I consider myself an atheist. I was never a religious person, even though my father was very religious. I don't pray and never have, but my father never missed *namaz* [prayer] or any other religious rituals. I'm not totally an atheist, I do believe God exists, but I don't perform any religious rituals. As a family tradition, though, we all gather together on Ramadan. All my children visit me then.

I went to the local school in my village. I liked attending school, and always tried to devote most of my time to studying. We studied math, literature and so on. Literature was my favorite subject. I don't remember if it was in school or in university, but I was a very active participant in the literature and drama clubs.

I was sent to the army when I was 18 years old. My father was no longer with us at that time; he had died when I was eight. Certainly, my mother and sisters had a hard time without a man around. [In the army, he was given an award for bravery on Nov. 14, 1944.]

From 1947 to 1949, I studied at the Osh State Teachers' Institute, in the Kyrgyz Language and Literature Department. After graduation, from 1951 to 1956, I went to the M. Gorky Literature Institute in Moscow.

I remember when Stalin died. I was already back in Kyrgyzstan. Everybody was in a great pain, including me. I even started to smoke, but after two packs of cigarettes, I couldn't handle it any more.

I was married twice. My first wife passed away because of health problems. I did not steal either of my wives. We already knew each other and we got married by mutual agreement. I have three daughters and one son.

I moved to the city [Bishkek] in 1957, when Chingis Aitmatov and several other poets and artists, including me, were given these apartments [in the building where the interview took place]. These apartments are the only apartments in Kyrgyzstan that were set aside for artists. For entertainment, I like to read a lot. I like to stay home alone with my books and write new poems.

Kyrgyz food has not changed over my lifetime, but my eating habits have changed a lot because I'm diabetic. I am on a very strict diet. I have my breakfast at 8 a.m., follower by tea with powdered milk at 11 a.m. Exactly at 1 p.m., I have lunch. Usually, I have only one dish for lunch: soup, most of the time. At 3 p.m. and at 5 p.m. I have tea with milk again. Then I have dinner at 8 p.m. and, finally, yogurt before bed. For dinner, I usually eat meat, fish, lamb, or chicken.

For almost half a year, I've been on this diet, which

includes a lot of dairy products. But I also like to eat pastas, soups, *lagman*, and Uzbek *shashlyk*.[51] The only thing that I avoid buying is street food. I consider it unhealthy and unsanitary. You never know what kind of meat is used in it. Basically, I like everything my daughters cook for me. My family only eats out sometimes, during celebrations like weddings, birthdays, and family parties. And that's the only time I drink alcohol — during big celebrations. Recently, I allowed myself to do it during the Nooruz[52] holiday.

My first language was Kyrgyz; my parents spoke Kyrgyz. I also speak Russian. Before the army, I couldn't speak any Russian, but then I learned it and now I speak perfect Russian. I use both Russian and Kyrgyz at home and at work. My first poem was in Kyrgyz. I wrote it when I was in the army. Fifteen of my books are written in Russian. About 30 of my other books are in Kyrgyz. I've translated works by Pushkin, [Sergei] Yesenin, Shakespeare, Lermontov, Omar Khayyam and other famous writers into Kyrgyz.

When I was young, I rarely heard people speaking Kyrgyz to each other. However, when I go out to walk in the parks now, most of the people are speaking to each other in Kyrgyz. In my opinion, Kyrgyz is used much more widely now than it was in Soviet times.

[Jusuyev's books in Russian include: "*V ozhdanii gostya,*" "*Orlitsa,*" "*Gorni zori,*" and "*Zhavoronok.*" His poem "Kanat and Zarina" has been adapted for the stage and for film.]

[Jusuyev has won many awards for his writing, including: a "diploma" from the High Council of the Kyrgyz SSR (1966); a

---

[51] *Shashlyk* is meat grilled on skewers, generally over a charcoal fire, often marinated or spiced.

[52] *Nooruz* is the traditional Persian new year celebration, which falls on the first day of spring. It is a major holiday in Kyrgyzstan and throughout Central Asia.

"diploma" from the High Council of Yakutia (1996); a "diploma" from the High Council of Ukraine (1974); the "Dank" medal for efforts in the development of culture and art in Kyrgyzstan (1997); the title of "national poet of Kyrgyzstan" (1981); the title of "honored person of the Kyrgyz Republic" (1995); the Toktogul national prize (1998); and the Manas award granted by the president of the Kyrgyz Republic (2000). Also, schools in Say-Talaa, Kara-Luljin, Jarooz, and Kara-Suyskiy are named after him.]

29. The Driver

Pyotr Federovich Melenkov, who is Russian, was born in 1936 in the village of Admovka, Russia. After serving in the army, he settled in southern Kyrgyzstan, where he started a family and worked for many years as a driver for an antimony[53] plant. Akylbek Baltabaev interviewed him in the town of Kadamjai, in Batken oblast [province], Kyrgyzstan, on March 9-10, 2009.

I lived in Orenburg *oblast* [province], in the village of Admovka. My parents were Fedor Ivanovich Malenkov and Natalia Sergeevna Malenkova. My first memories begin in 1939.

We lived on a collective farm. Life was very difficult; people were living very badly. Still, they were friendly to each other. In general, there was a really joyful mood on the collective farm. Everyone tried to help each other. People kind of believed in God and that helped them, too.

I am Christian, but I respect all the other religions. I don't really practice my religion, but I believe in God. I have only been to church a few times in my life. The first time was when I was christened. After that, my parents told me what God was and all that sort of thing. When I was young, the older people went to churches, but the younger ones did not. But, as people get older, they become more attracted to religion.

People of many different nationalities lived in our village. There was a really friendly atmosphere. For example, I had a friend — at that time we were really young — he was Kazakh and his family was the only Kazakh family in our village. His dad used to be a shepherd. But back then, we didn't even think about what nationalities we were. We were young and we used to just play together. I know now that people discriminate against each other. But back in those times, no one would dis-

---

[53] Antimony is used in batteries, matches, paints, ceramics, enamels, electronics, rubber, and a wide variety of alloys, including pewter.

criminate against anyone.

Anyway, I remember one day we were playing. I don't know how old I was — maybe about eight years old. I had not started school yet. I don't even remember my friend's name now. I know that he was Kazakh, though. We went to his house. It was about five houses away from where I lived. His family was going to have lunch or breakfast, I don't remember. Anyway, his dad told him to ask me to join them, but I was shy and did not want to sit with them, so I ran away. Of course, his parents were offended. Later, I saw my friend again and we started playing and he said: "My dad asked me, 'What kind of friend do you have, who can act like that?'" Well, I listened to him and, next time I went to their house we all ate at one table. This is the kind of childhood I had.

Later, in 1941, the war began. Many of our "village-mates" were taken into the army to fight the enemy. Everyone said that they were defending their homeland and that, eventually, they would overcome the enemy. Though I was young, I understood the situation. I remember when my uncle hugged me — he was leaving, too. Everyone was crying. The old people were telling the young men to come back victorious.

It was really hard to see our relatives and our "village-mates" leaving. We lived in a place where public transportation was rare and I remember seeing the Siberians pass by. Some were on foot, some were skiing. At that time I thought they were going hunting, but now I know that they were going to fight, because they were dressed warmly, in sheepskin jackets. It was winter. They were in a really joyful mood, ready to overcome the enemy. Some were also traveling in vehicles and on sleds drawn by horses. People met them and walked with them. Even if they were strangers, we treated them like we knew them. Everyone was in the mood to beat the enemy in so we could live in peace and friendship.

And there so many different nationalities. I did not know at that time that our country was multinational. I learned in school that our country was very big and multinational. For example, I remember from school that we had 60,000 kilometers [37,282 miles] of land borders and that the distance from west to east, from the European border to Anadyr, Chukotka [in the extreme northeast of Russia] was 11,000 kilometers [6,835 miles].

There were great hardships during the war. Listen to me, my dear 'grandson,' we had to eat everything. We had to eat everything, from grass to mushrooms. We had to eat grass you know [tears looming]. But I don't want to talk about it — it is all over now. But, yes, we had to eat everything. People were just trying to live and do everything to find a way to live better the next day. Women, old men and children stayed at home. They plowed the land themselves, mostly. There were no tractors. People even harnessed cows to their plows. The bulls had been driven to the front to help feed the army. Back then, I didn't think much about the Germans because I was too young. What could a five-year-old kid think?

Of course, there was some hatred towards the enemy. When the war was on the verge of ending, of course, we had negative feelings towards Germans. My wife told me that in their village, they had a wounded Soviet soldier and a German prisoner of war. When the German first arrived, he asked for some food and our people fed him. Then the Soviet soldier lost his arm [because of his wounds] and one woman told the German soldier, angrily: "Look what you've done." And, after that, the wounded Soviet soldier stood up and said: "Give him something to eat. He is a soldier, just like I am. He was executing orders, just like I was."

Even though the Germans were our enemies, I think they are the same as we are. They did not want to do anything bad to us. It was just politicians that stirred them up against other nations. That kind of thing needs to stop. We should live in friendship and peace.

For instance, let's take the earthquake in Tashkent.[54] It felt so good to see people from all the republics of our country come to restore the city. Ukrainians, Belarusians, and people from the Baltics were there — I mean people from all over the country. When there were earthquakes in Almaty and in Ashgabat, many people went to reconstruct those cities, too.

Anyway, finally, victory day came. I remember one teacher at school. Her name was Grafina Ivanovna Malenkova —she had the same last name as me — and that day she was so happy, announcing: "Victory! Victory!" I think she is still alive. Happy people ran out into the streets cheering.

Some people say that Stalin was bad. Yes, I agree that there was some cruelty, but he could not check on everybody — it was impossible. And people are right to be offended by what happened. But I liked one thing about him: he did not mess up and pull the country down. Once, Hitler said: "All I need to do is to enter Russia and they will run away like dogs." How humiliating that was. However, the people of the USSR did not run away; they beat the enemy. And now, though we are at peace, our leaders are bringing the country down.

Twenty million people died during the war. Now look at the number who have died because of democracy. I think it is even more than in the Great Patriotic War. For example, as I remember Nagorno-Karabakh, Chechnya, and Pridnestrovie,[55] are the places where such things happened. Can you imagine [tears come to Malenkov's eyes]? When I talk about these things, I get so frustrated. Back then, people used to say that Russia was the older brother [in the Soviet Union], but I never said that. I treated everyone equally.

---

[54] In 1966, Tashkent was hit by an earthquake that measured 7.5 on the Richter scale.

[55] Also known as Transnistria or Trans-Dneister; formerly part of Moldova.

Back then we worked for the government and the government worked for us. I am still shocked that the Soviet people have changed so drastically after the fall of the Soviet Union. They are always trying to grab something now. They have become disrespectful. People say that it's caused by business. Back then, people were working for the country and the country worked for the people.

I used to drive the route from Kadamjai to Minsk [Belarus] and back. From Minsk to Kadamjai is 5,600 kilometers. It was wonderful to drive all the way home from Minsk. I would feel so nice, deep in my heart, that I would sing lines from Mayakovskiy: *Shiroka strana moya rodnaya, mnogo v nei lesov, polei i rek, ya takoi drugoi strany ne znayu, gde tak volno dyshit chelovek* [my country is very big, there are many forests, lands and rivers in it, I don't know any other country where man could breathe freely like this].These are good words; they matched the situation.

Parents, leaders and teachers always taught us to respect people. Now people say bad things about Stalin and other people. I think it's true that Stalin treated war prisoners severely.

Their lives in concentration camps were cruel and Stalin said: "We don't have war prisoners, we have traitors to our motherland." It's easy to criticize this now, but maybe it was right the right thing to do back then, during the war. Anyway, the Soviet people got through the war and I think the current CIS countries will eventually reunite and live in peace.

Many did not return from the war, though. Some lost fathers, some lost sons, etc. After the war, the recovery began. Even though we were little kids, we did our best to help the country recover from the war. Those were very happy times. Everyone was trying to help by working on the collective farm. Fathers and grandfathers used to tell us: "Now that we've beaten the enemy, we'll have much better lives." Everyone was doing their part to help develop the country.

We grew rye, wheat, corn, and sunflowers. And it all went to the state. On our collective farm, we harvested the crops by hand, with sickles. In the Soviet era, if you had one cow and two sheep, you were considered a rich man. But if you did not, you weren't, so people wanted to united into collective farms. It was not bad. The bad thing was that people did not quite understand what a collective farm was. That's why they didn't want to join collective farms. It was actually easier to work that way — it just required honesty.

We had a planned economy back then. Look at it now. For example we don't have a heating system and the electricity is always shutting off. During the Soviet era, the electricity was never shut down. If the electric plant paused for an hour, it would have been reported to Moscow and the people who were guilty would have been punished. Now we want to copy West, but it isn't working for us, because we are not ready for it. If you are building a house, you have to have all the materials: cement, sand, bricks. If you don't have one of those elements, you cannot build a house. Maybe privatization is good in general, but Kyrgyzstan was not ready for it.

I remember, after the war, we harvested the crops with horse drawn vehicles. I remember Uncle Styopa harnessing horses, since there were no trucks or other machines. Once we'd gathered the crops, we would take them to the grain elevator. Then the grain went to the district center. There, [the mayor] would meet them and he would say: "Oh dear *kolhozniks* [collective farmers], thank you for bringing us the harvest! You yourselves ate and brought some for us, too!" Later, we began to live better. We received trucks when I was older and was helping to load the crops into the grain elevator. So this is how it was to live at that time: difficult but very friendly and happy.

I went to school in our village. My first teacher was Aleksandra Ivanovna Isaeva. Once I had finished the first grade and entered the second grade, my mother died. That's when I started having problems. My grades fell and I missed my mother a lot. The cemetery was located just across from our school and I could see it and I didn't listen to what was being said in class much. I just looked at the place where my mother was buried. It was really hard for me. I wanted to become an adult faster so I could start working.

We studied Russian, literature, botany, geography, natural science, etc. When I read a book I always had a map open in front of me, so I could see where the place I was reading about was located. For instance, I was reading a book called *Wilderness of the North*, and I had a map and found the place that book was about. I think it was somewhere in Canada. So I know maps really well.

My first teacher taught me from first grade to fourth grade. She taught me to respect other nations because we had a multi-national country. I remember our principal taught Constitution and history. Her name was Antonina Kirillovna. Grafina Ivanovna taught geography. Korney Borisovich, who was a very old German man — probably 70 years old — taught math and he was a very kind and respectful man. After my mother died, my math was terrible. One day Korney Borisovich called me up and said: "Come to my house some time and I will teach you some math." After that, my math got better. But my Russian was still really bad.

My parents spoke only in Russian. In school, we studied in Russian and, as a foreign language, we studied German, which Korney Borisovich taught us. Now, I know Kyrgyz and a little bit of Uzbek, too, but not much.

I used to get up in the morning and wash myself. I would have breakfast and then my parents went to the collective farm and we did the chores all by ourselves. Then I went to school. The classes lasted for 45 minutes and then the bell rang and there was a five-minute break and then it was time to go back to school. After the third period, we had a big break to eat. It lasted for 15 minutes. I finished only seven classes because, after World War II, life was difficult and people lacked the funds for education. People tried to work, rather than study.

I was still in school when I heard Stalin had died. It was announced on the radio. We had really bad radio reception, but we could still hear what they were saying. When we heard about his death, we all cried. Everybody wondered how we were going to live without Stalin. Stalin was considered the father of the people. People at school, old and young were crying and saying that their leader had died. I was born during Lenin's regime, but I grew up during Stalin's.

Then I served in the army. I was drafted in 1955 and sent to Central Asia. I've been living in Central Asia ever since. I served in the army in the Turkestan district [Turkmenistan]: Ashgabat, Mary; near the mountains, in the desert. And wherever I served, I would meet good Soviet people. All the people I met during my army days were kind and hospitable.

I also served in the Caucasus, in Bakinskiy district, in anti-aircraft defense. I met many good people there, too, who treated me like I was their son. In the army there was no violence against young conscripts. Serving in the army was very pleasant for me. There were people of many nationalities, even Jews. Everyone was trying to defend our country and there were no hostilities among any nationalities. We were taught to respect and love everyone on the planet. In the army, I worked as a driver and, after I got out of the army, I worked for 42 years as a driver.

After the army, I went to Central Asia and ended up in Kadamjai. This is how it happened: When we were coming back from the army, I met a man. He was returning from his unit and I was returning from mine. I sailed with him on a boat [across the Caspian Sea] from Baku [Azerbaijan] to Krasnovodsk [Turkmenistan] and from Krasnovodsk we took the train.

Everyone was friendly and almost everyone was going to Central Asia. There were Kyrgyz, Kazakhs, Uzbeks — there were as many nationalities as we had in the whole country.

So I made friends with this guy and he said to me: "Let's go to Kadamjai, you'll find work there, we have jobs. You can work as a driver, we have very pleasant weather, and the people are very nice." So he persuaded me to come to Kadamjai. On the way, we changed trains in Ursatevsk and headed to Andijan. We arrived in Fergana and from Fergana, we went to Vodil [in Uzbekistan, on the Kyrgyz border]. He said he had some relatives there and decided to drop by and suggested I go with him. But I said that I had to go before it got really dark because I had to find some place to stay in Kadamjai. So he stopped there [in Vodil] and we arranged to meet in the military registration and enlistment office when he got to Kadamjai. That was some time in 1958. I never saw him again.

When I arrived, I tried to find some people that I knew. Finally, after running around from office to office, I found one guy I knew. Then I got a job. I thought, well I will work for a while and then go back home, to Orenburg. On the first day of work my boss came up to me and said: "Here is a truck, fix it, run it, and take it tomorrow for yourself." I said, "What about tools?" There weren't even enough tools. I collected the tools gradually, over time. I bought some in the market and some were given to me. I have lived here for 50 years now.

During the Soviet period, we lived well. I was not a Communist, but I respected their discipline. I always respected my job and have always been rewarded for it: I was given bonuses, certificates for safe driving, a national badge, and also some medals. But, right now, my life has gotten really difficult. It is very difficult to make living now. The people need to unite. Alright, we will keep the names — Uzbekistan, Kyrgyzstan, etc. — but let's just get united like in the good old days. We don't need hostility or war. We have to ensure that the sky will be clear above the heads of our grandsons.

We had almost everything in our shops during the Soviet times, the so-called "era of stagnation." For pensioners these times are really hard. During the Soviet era, you could go to a *stolovaya* [cafeteria] and eat and have sweet tea for only two *kopeks* [pennies]. Bread was free; there was a sign on the wall above the bread: "Take as much as you can eat." It would cost about 10 *ruble*s to get down to Fergana and come back with a backpack full of groceries. Or, for instance, if I wanted to go to my homeland — and my homeland is 2,039 kilometers from Kadamjai — it would cost 19 *ruble*s to take the train from Andijan and a plane ticket would cost 42 *ruble*s.

In Soviet times, I could afford anything for myself. I could buy everything I wanted. If I wanted vodka, I would buy it. If I wanted cognac, I would buy it. I always had cognac at home. We used to arrange concerts at the factory. Every factory department had its own creative group, which would give performances. We even went to Bishkek, when it was called Frunze. We played soccer sometimes. The first time I ever watched TV was when I was in the army. The soldiers collected money among themselves and bought a TV. It was in 1957, in Baku. Before that, we just had radios.

Women have always played a huge role in the family. A wife must understand many things to keep the family stable. If the wife understands, any disagreement can easily be settled. For example, I lived with my wife for 49 years, always in peace. We solved all our problems together. We never had inequalities. Neither her parents nor my parents interfered with our lives. When we had kids, life became even more fun.

My whole my family is living abroad now. My children and grandchildren are all working or studying abroad. There's one in Belarus and the others are in Russia. When my son graduated from university, he wanted to stay here and live here, but he couldn't find a job, so he had to stay in Russia. My son helps me, but I try to live without his help. They have their own problems and I think I should not be dependent on them. But when I need something, I ask.

Even if people are leaving Kyrgyzstan, going abroad, and changing their citizenships, they still miss their homeland; their souls still live in their motherlands. For example, sometimes I want to go back to my homeland, where I was born. Sometimes I criticize myself for having left my homeland. I should have built a house there and lived there. On the other, moving abroad helps people. There are not enough jobs, so what can people do? When they are abroad they can earn money and support their families. It is good for the country, too.

I live alone now and it is boring. My brother used to live here, too, but he left to return to our homeland. He was there for two years and then he died. I remember he wrote to me once, telling me not to come to our homeland because the change of climate would stress my body. But how can I live by myself? My kids come sometimes, but then they leave again. I am happy that they are able to come and visit me. My son graduated from university and is working now.

So I live alone and I cook *plov* [lamb pilaf], *borscht* [beet and cabbage soup], and *kasha* [cream of wheat] for myself. I don't buy meat often because it is expensive. But, sometimes, when I can afford to eat meat, I do. I have to budget my spending because I have to pay for electricity, natural gas, and utility payments, as well. I am not saying that it is too hard to live these days, but we still have to work to survive. Luckily, we are from a generation that does not fear obstacles.

30. The Propagandist

Erjigit Shakirov, who is Kyrgyz, was born in 1931 in the village of Okhna in the Kadamjai district of in Batken oblast [province], Kyrgyzstan. "We studied Russian history because there were no materials about Kyrgyz history ... We didn't know our own history," he recalled. Akylbek Baltabaev interviewed him there on March 11, 2009.

There was hardship during the war, of course. As a substitute for food, we had soup made from flour and water. We ate boiled *kefir* during the war. There was almost no meat. Sometimes we just ate bread with tea. I remember one man had a wedding and, at the wedding, the main food they had was *plov* [lamb pilaf]. One little boy who had never seen rice in his life — until that day he had eaten only boiled flour — was given *plov* at that wedding party. He didn't eat the rice, he just scattered it around; he wanted to eat his usual boiled flour. Along with the rice, he also tossed away the bread and meat, since he had never seen them either. He screamed, demanding his *atala* — this is what we called flour soup. His father was disgraced in front of everyone there. People yelled at him to leave the wedding. He put his son on his donkey and took him home.

That boy did not know what bread, meat or rice were. But now, life is much better. People have everything they need. They have vegetables and fruits. Now we eat soups like *shorpa* and *ystyk*. From time to time, we eat rice with meat. We also eat *manty* [steamed dumplings] sometimes.

Of course, back then, everyone hated Germans. People used to sing songs about Germans. In 1947, German prisoners of war were transported here and I saw them. I went to school in Halmion [25 km from Kadamjai]. Our teacher took us to where the Germans lived and worked — in a colony. Their culture was totally different from ours. They built houses there and lived in them. They wore uniforms. The government criticized the Germans and their capitalism in the propaganda and in the press. But the Germans near us were not abused at all.

I started school here in Okhna in 1940 at the age of nine. I finished seventh grade in 1946. There was no secondary school in our village. The only secondary school was in Halmion. I went there and graduated from it in 1949. It was the post-war period and life was tough. There was no dormitory. Students slept in hay. We would lay down the hay and then put a piece of tarpaulin over it and sleep there. A few years later, though, when things got better, we got beds to sleep on.

We studied the same subjects as students do now: Kyrgyz, Russian, math, chemistry, and physics. We didn't have any foreign language classes because we didn't have anyone who could teach foreign languages. Our teachers were of many different nationalities: Tatars, Uzbeks, Russians, and Uyghurs. We had a shortage of Kyrgyz language teachers, so our Kyrgyz language teacher was Tatar.

Classes began at 9 a.m. and they ended at 1 p.m. I was good at geography and history. I was good at maps, too. That helped me when I entered the institute. I could navigate any map. I could find any place on any map. I wasn't good at math, though. I majored in history at the institute. We studied Russian history because there were no materials about Kyrgyz history. There was nothing about the history of other nationalities, either. We didn't know our own history, but we knew Russian history very well. Today, we have Kyrgyz history classes.

Before collectivization, my grandparents had their own land. During collectivization, though, everyone's land became part of the collective farm. After the *kolkhoz* [collective farm] disappeared, the land was given back to the families that had been part of the *kolkhoz*. Each family got 2,500 square meters. Then the *sovhoz* [state farm] was created, and each family was given 800 square meters of land. We grew potatoes and corn.

We bred livestock. Our uncles grew apples and apricots. They did not sell them. They just grew them for us. We never bought fruits or vegetables in the bazaar. We ate dried apricots in the winter, we used to make flour out of dried apples.

In Soviet times if you grew something, you did it for your country. Now, if you grow anything, you do it only for yourself. Collectivization was good, but we did not have enough land. There needs to be a lot of land for collectivization to work. Some people benefited from privatization and some got nothing. For example, we did not receive any [useful] land during privatization. We received 200 square meters of land after the collapse of the Soviet Union and that land is somewhere in the middle of nowhere where you can't grow anything. It's too far away — we can't get the machinery there and there's no irrigation. The people who got good land, where you can grow something, benefited from privatization.

There were Chechens resettled here; some Ingush and Balkars were also resettled here.[56] The Chechens received houses here and lived in them. They lived a good life. Nobody tried to do anything to them. Everyone had the same amount of food. Land was given to everybody. Also, Jews and Poles were resettled here. Then those who had been resettled left.

At first the Chechens stayed. But they left, too, after Stalin's death. The government resettled these people because, if they were close to the front line [during World War II], they would have helped the enemy.

In 1949, after I finished high school, I entered the Fergana Pedagogical Institute. I graduated from it in 1953 and worked in Uzbekistan for two years. I was the only person from our whole district with a higher education. Then, in 1954, some others joined me. From 1956 until 2000, I worked here in Okhna, in our school. While I was working here, I participated

---

[56] In 1944, Stalin had all the Chechens, Balkars, and Ingush deported from the Caucasus to Kazakhstan and Kyrgyzstan.

in many social activities. I worked as a lecturer for our Frunze Party Committee. Later, I worked as a propagandist in the Kadamjai party organization during the *sovhoz* [state farm] times. In 1990, we opened a memorial museum for Abdykadyr Orozbekov,[57] who was chairman of the central executive committee of Kyrgyz SSR [and was from Okhna]. Then we opened a historical museum in the Okhna secondary school. In 1985, I was recognized as a distinguished teacher of the Kyrgyz SSR. In 2003 I was given the status of "national teacher." I worked at the school for 50 years.

We are all Muslims. Compared to Uzbeks, Kyrgyz people were not very religious in the past. But now we have become more religious. There was no mosque here during the Soviet period; the government was against religion. Now there are many mosques. There is at least one mosque in each village. During the Soviet period, there was no freedom of religion. Religious people were persecuted. People couldn't pray. Mosques were turned into storehouses and schools and sometimes they were just destroyed. Some people believed so deeply, though, that they would celebrate Muslim holidays in spite of the government.

In the Soviet days, women mostly worked on *sovhoz*es, growing tobacco. Now women work more than men. They are doctors and teachers, etc. The role of women has increased today. During the Soviet times, men were the main power. They did the hard work. Back then, children often did not go to school. Instead, they picked cotton and did other farm work. They were forced to do it. I remember when I was a teacher, we

---

[57] Orozbekov (1889-1938), born in Okhna, was a baker until the revolution in 1917. During the civil war, he rose in the Red Army from private to commander to commissar. Then he became active in politics and, in 1927, he became the chairman of the TsIK of what was then the Kyrgyz Autonomous Soviet Socialist Republic. In 1937, he was arrested and sentenced to be shot, but he got sick the next year and died. In 1956 he was "rehabilitated" and there is now a street named after him in Bishkek.

used to take pupils out into the fields until December. In the summer, we used to take them to mow grass. There is nothing like that now. Back then, if they refused to go they would be held responsible for it and the militia would come and prosecute them.

Back in those days, there was no love. Arranged marriages were very common. Our parents would arrange marriages and that's how we got married. We didn't even see each other before the wedding. For example, I hadn't ever seen my wife until our marriage. Our parents arranged it. I was 23 and she was 18. Now I have eight kids and four of them have received higher educations and three of them have received technical educations.

31. The Hero

Syinanbyubyu Namatova, who is Kyrgyz, was born in 1936 in the village of Dzhail, near Kara Balta, Kyrgyzstan. "In 1969, I met Brezhnev and he presented me with a Volga GAS 24 car as a reward for my good work," she recalled. Maksat Nepesov interviewed her in the village of Ak Bashat [Sosnovka] on March 20, 2009.

My name is Syinanbyubyu. I was born on March 8, 1936, in the village of Dzhail, near Kara Balta. Earlier [in the Soviet era], the village was called Bolshevik.

My childhood was very nice. I never worked on a farm; my parents raised horses. For my first six years in school, I studied on the *kolkhoz* [collective farm]. Then I moved to Bishkek to live with my relatives because my parents were engaged in stockbreeding so they did not stay in one place — they often wandered. My parents had more than 100 horses on their farm. I graduated from Bishkek's School No. 1. At school, I studied well but I don't remember what marks I got or what subjects I liked the most.

At that time Russian was considered the most prestigious language. I know three languages: Russian, Kyrgyz, and German, but I've already forgotten German. I know Russian because I studied with Russian children in Bishkek. In the capital, there were a lot of Russian-speaking people.

My university years in Leningrad were also good. I lived without a care in the world, had fun, and relaxed. I studied at thetextile university in Leningrad and I graduated from there. I had two girlfriends in Leningrad. One was called Lera. At that time she was married, but after some years her relatives told me that she had died. My years as a student were carefree and very cheerful. My hobbies were singing and dancing. We sang a lot of Russian songs.

I got married in 1955. I was 19 years old. It was arranged by our parents. My husband worked as a teacher. I went to work at a factory called "40 Years of October" [in Bishkek]. We made clothing there. I started out as a young technologist and I worked there for 13 years. Now that factory is gone. Instead, there is a shopping center called Silk Way.

I spent many years in Bishkek. My family was well off. We had a good, two-story house in Bishkek. I remember that there was a shop nearby. The house was located near a mosque, at the intersection of Moscow and Gogol streets. Then my father forced us to move to a collective farm and, with my family, we moved to Sosnovka in 1965. I threw everything away and moved to the village. My life changed. I began to work as a shepherd — I did that for 15 years. During that time, the *kolkhoz* [collective farm] helped us a lot.

It was very hard to move from Bishkek to the village. In the city, especially in the capital, everything is always clean. In the village, everything is dirty. It was hard, but I got used to it. Now I think, if a person is healthy, it is better for him to live in the village, because there is milk, meat, cabbage, and tomatoes and it's all natural and available. We grow everything ourselves. But if you live in a city, you can't keep everything in your refrigerator — you have to go to the market. Here, you can just go out to the yard, pick something, wash it, and eat it. Now, certainly, in my old age, I don't need anything. The main thing that I need is calmness. Therefore, I think it is better to live in the village.

In 1969, I met Brezhnev and he presented me with a Volga GAS 24 car as a reward for my good work. I was a hero of the Ninth Five-Year Plan. I traveled all over the USSR. I visited Bulgaria, Czechoslovakia, and Germany. During the Soviet era, it was possible to travel easily.

I was a Communist and an intelligent woman. To be a Communist means to be fair and to be responsible for everything that those who have more senior posts tell you to do and to always be alert. In that time, there was very strict control from Moscow. I think it was good. People were more obedient.

Earlier, you were at work all day and, in the evening, you went home. Now people do not know what to do.

I've always been a Muslim. Even when I was a Communist, I never let go of my Muslim beliefs. I still prayed to God, just as I had since I was a child, although, in the Soviet days, if you even said "God," it was bad and you could sometimes be punished. Nowadays there are more believers than there were in the Soviet period because, in the Soviet period, the Communists did not allow people to be believers. I'm a Muslim, but I do not pray — I simply believe in God. But I also celebrate many Muslim holidays. For example, on Ramadan, I fast. But for the past two years, I did not fast because I am already old and have a problem with my stomach. In my family, nobody went to religious school. I always pass young men at religious schools and wish them all the best and, as their elder, give them lots of useful and clever advice.

My favorite dish is *beshbarmak*. Here is how we prepare this dish: we raise a sheep for a month or two in a special way and then we kill it, salt it, and keep it for the right amount of time. Then we cut off a piece of meat, throw it in a pot, and boil it for two hours. We cook the noodles separately. Then we cut the meat up into small slices and we add the noodles and onions and pepper to taste.

I can also tell you about Stalin, Andropov, and many other influential people of that time. Stalin and Andropov were very decent people and wielded power effectively. People understood and obeyed them. Now our president [Kurmanbek

Bakiyev] issues orders and nobody obeys. If there is rigid control, everything is good. Everyone knows his duty and how to conduct himself. I also remember Khrushchev's times. I lived in the city and my brother and sister were students and, in the morning, they would go and stand in lines for three or four hours to buy bread. We had money, but it was difficult to buy anything. And the regime was getting softer and the controls weren't so strict and rigid. In Brezhnev's time, things got better.

Now, in Bakiyev's time, there are many criminals. If he was just more strict and rigid, things would be good in this country. It is very bad that the Soviet Union has broken up. If we still had the Soviet Union, everything would be very good. Now the youth have become lazy — they are all idlers, not like we were in the past. Back then, if you did not work for three days, you would be forced to work. At that time, everyone worked or studied. Now the majority of the young people don't work and don't study. They just live on their parents' money. For example, I remember, my grandmother, who was 103 years old, called me once at 3 a.m. and asked me to come see her at her home. I arrived before 10 a.m. that same morning. But these days, I don't think my children would arrive so quickly if I asked them to come see me.

My mother died in 1985. My father died in 1996. My husband died in 2007. I have seven children and all my children are educated. My oldest son works as a tractor driver. My second son is a military man, a colonel, who lives in Kant. One of my daughters works as a bookkeeper for the Ministry of Internal Affairs in Bishkek. My children always help me financially. My grandsons have already finished school — some of them have already graduated from universities and many of them have already married. I have 14 great-grandchildren and 20 grandchildren. My grandchildren study at KNU [Kyrgyz National University] and at KTU [Kyrgyz Technical University].

Thanks to God, I have everything I need: food, clothing, and money. Now the main thing is money. In the past, it wasn't like that. Back then we thought only about how to live well and how to raise our children. My son, who lives here in the village, works as a tractor driver. He finished his time in the army and then he got a little bit spoiled and so I ordered him to leave everything and come to the village and, since then, he has worked as a tractor driver.

32. THE CONSERVATIVE

Oktiabr Akmoldoev, who is Kyrgyz, was born in 1939, in the semi-nomadic village of Kemer, in the Talas province of Kyrgyzstan. During the collectivization drive, he and the rest of his village moved to a place near Ken-Aral and began a settled life. "I used to eat all my food with my hands, if possible. I still do. I can't taste the food if I don't eat it with my hands," he said. Murat Tuloberdiev interviewed him in the city of Talas on March 23, 2009.

The process of collectivization started before I was born. During collectivization, basically the Bolsheviks confiscated all the land, livestock, and other assets from the *bay-manap*s [the rich], and used them to create big *kolkhoz*es [collective farms] that belonged to everyone equally. I really supported — and still support — collectivization. During the years of collectivization, everyone became socially equal and the Kyrgyz people began to live settled lives, which led them to live more civilized lives.

During World War II, I was a little kid, but I still remember the difficult conditions of that time. Since my childhood coincided with the war, I did not have a typical childhood. All of my father's siblings had gone to the front and had not returned. My father did not go to war because he was assigned by the government to help build the Big Chui Canal. My mother had take care of me and my two brothers on her own. Like most other people in our village, we were concerned only with getting enough food and clothing.

I don't know about other parts of Kyrgyzstan, but in my village, during the war, we did not live a settled life. People used to live far apart from each other, in boz-uis [yurts]. Since all the strong men had gone to war, the village didn't have enough strong people to work. People became more integrated, more caring. I guess they only survived the hardships of that time because of their cooperation. So, I guess hard times create integrity, make people sympathetic and helpful.

During the war, people had to eat some foods — if you consider them as foods — that they would not have eaten otherwise. There were cases when people had to gather grasshoppers, fry them and eat them. And sometimes people ate eat *atkulaks* [wild grass] root. The government was unable to deal with our problems — its only concern was defeating the Germans. So people found ways to survive on their own.

People generally hated the Germans after the war, because they were viewed as occupiers. But lately, especially after the collapse of the Soviet Union, the attitude has been changing dramatically. As we analyze our lives, we see that the Germans were good for us. We learned many things from them. They shared their experience and knowledge with us — they taught us a lot.

There were some peoples, like Karachays, Chechens, and Kalmyks, that had betrayed the Soviet Union and cooperated with Nazi Germany. So Stalin confiscated their properties and sent them to Central Asia. I think Stalin thought of us as barbarians, as wild people. So he thought that if he sent traitors to these regions, they would disperse among the barbarian people somehow. Some of the children of the forced migrants died just as they were arriving in our village. They didn't have clothes and they were so hungry that it seemed like they could eat us. Our village showed them hospitality. We shared our homes with them.

During the reconstruction years, life got better — but it did not happen all of a sudden. Life was still difficult. Many men did not return from the war, which meant that old people, women, and children, had to work. There was not really any equipment until 1960s, so almost all the agricultural work was done by hand. We heard that during the war and after the war, some industries were being moved from the western part of the USSR to Central Asia, but no industry was moved to our village, or even to Talas *oblast* [province]. That's probably because there was no railroad in Talas oblast and, without a railroad, it would have been difficult to transport industrial goods to and from our region.

Stalin died on March 5, 1953. We were at school when we heard about it and all the students put black strips of material on their clothes and cried for about an hour. Some students even continued crying when they got home. During those years, Stalin was thought of as an ideal leader. People deeply believed that we had won the war thanks his competence and wisdom. Some young people felt closer to Stalin than to their parents. He was like our collective father. We used to sing songs about Stalin and those songs became like anthems. That's why, when he passed away, people were so full of sorrow, as if one of their close relatives had died.

There was only one elementary school in our village. I studied there for four years and then I had to go to a neighboring village, Ken-Aral. Every day, we had to walk more than three kilometers to the school and back. At that time, being a student was very important. As a result of the war, only about one person from each street was literate. So, being educated was very fashionable. Those who were educated were respected. Despite the lack of supplies and reading and writing materials, students did everything they could to study. For them, being a student meant deepening their knowledge, widening their outlook, learning about the world outside of their village, and learning about their history.

Every day we had four classes and each class lasted for 45 minutes. During the breaks between classes, everybody used to run out of the school to play. There were so few students in each class that the teachers had more than enough time to question every student every day. We studied Kyrgyz, Russian, math, algebra, German, geography, and history. My favorite classes were history and geography. From history, we learned about our past and from geography, we learned about places outside our village. I learned two basic things at school: how to write and how to read. These two things have been useful throughout my life. Unfortunately, because of my circumstances, I was not able to go to university.

After Stalin died, Malikov became the First Secretary and then Bublin. Neither of them served for even one full year. Then Khrushchev took over. I didn't think he was a famous politician. I couldn't understand how he came to power. He served from 1955-1965 and, under his leadership, I remember, corn was brought from the US and the Soviet Union started growing it on a massive scale.

I started working on our *kolkhoz* when I was 14. We mostly grew wheat, tobacco, barley, and corn. There have been two major changes in agriculture since then. First, we have changed what we grow. When I was a child, we did not grow things like cabbage and potatoes. Now we grow both, and a lot of other new things. Second, we have adopted new techniques and technologies. Before 1955 people still used to use horses to pull handmade plows. It was only after 1955 that tractors and combines appeared.

I served in the army and, after returning, I went to work as a driver. It was while I was working as a driver that I met my future wife, Janyl. We dated for a while and liked each other, so I went to her parents to arrange our marriage. We have been living together ever since. We raised three children, all of whom are now married with children.

In the past, families used to be stronger and healthier. Families had integrity. Not only families, but entire neighborhoods used to live like big families. Now there is the idea that everyone is control of his own life. As a result, everybody is concerned with finding his or her own path, which has brought the idea of individualism into family life. I think only nice people can make strong, healthy families. First of all, it depends on their ancestors. If their ancestors were good people, they can bring up a good family. It is also important that parents teach their children good behavior and strong morals. If their children cannot resist negative influences, then there is little chance that they will build strong, healthy familes in the future.

Before the establishment of the Soviet government, women's lives were limited. A woman's job was to have babies, make food, and clean the house. All the outside work was done by husbands or fathers. Women did not have rights in Kyrgyz society. They did not have the right to divorce their husbands. They had to marry one of their husband's relatives if their husband died. Then women got equal rights and started taking part in public life, which left them less time for their families. They started getting jobs and earning almost as much as men, which made them independent of their husbands, financially. Now, after the collapse of the Soviet Union, women have become even more active in public life. Now we have deputies [in Parliament] and ministers [in government] who are women. Women have not traditionally done this kind of thing in Kyrgyz society, with the exception of Kurmanjan Datka, who served as the leader of the southern Kyrgyz tribes.

Where the role of men is concerned, we logically see the opposite effect, since they are the other half of the human race. If, in early times, families' outside affairs were handled by men, now women often do the outside work and their husbands stay home, taking care of their children and making food. The old social constraints have been dismantled and now whoever has the ability to make some money — whether husband or wife — works, and the other spouse stays home and takes care of the children.

In the past, young people used to do volunteer work for the government — projects on the *kolkhoz* [collective farm] or *sovkhoz* [state farm]. All work at that time was for the government, since there was no private sector. Now young people do not help the government voluntarily. They are all just looking to earn something for themselves. And it's not only the young people. The older generation is not concerned about public life anymore, either. We have lost our trust in the government and now everyone is on his own and cares only for himself.

During Soviet times, there was a lot of negative propaganda about the US — about the West in general. We used read in the press that — despite its claims — the US did not have democracy, that it was a place of aggression, inequality and slavery. But when we got access to information from outside the Soviet Union, we learned that what we had heard was not quite accurate. We realized that we were getting very biased information and that we had been indoctrinated. We had heard that the whites in America were making the blacks slaves, but now we have all witnessed how they elected a black man as their president. It seems like the best possibility for democracy is in the West, rather than in our homeland. I guess giving citizens inaccurate and negative information about the West was part of the constant rivalry between the USSR and the West.

During privatization, after the Soviet Union fell, all the assets of the *kolkhozi*, which had been considered the property of the people, were distributed to individual families. Some families were successful in managing their private farms, but most people had no idea what to do with their new land and animals. Some decided to merge into cooperatives to make their work more efficient and to pool their experience. Others absolutely could not figure out anything to do with their land, except to rent it to more successful farmers for a little bit of money. I really do not like privatization, I wish we could reconstitute the *kolkhozi* and *sovkhozi* so that all people would be equal again.

Since privatization, we have had problems with water. Now it is really hard to get water for your farm. The ones who can afford to bribe the water distribution authorities can get water without waiting their turns. Besides, now the farmers steal water from each other. For these reasons, it takes much longer to water your land than it did in the Soviet days. If we used to be able to water 100 hectares of land in about a week, now it's hard to finish watering 100 hectares of land in a month. Equipment is another problem. The rich people have bought all the farm equipment in the village and so the poor farmers have to wait until the rich farmers finish with their own lands before they can rent the equipment. Most of the time, poor farmers don't have the money to rent rich people's tractors and combines anyway, though.

When I was young, there were some people who believed in God in their hearts, but they could not be open about their faith in public, because practicing religion publicly would have led to their arrests. The government schools used to teach that there was no God. Still, religious people tried to abide by Sharia law and pray five times a day. They tried not to deceive people, not to have bad intentions, and not to steal. But they could not be open about practicing their religion. One of the Islamic traditions that did not erode, despite the Soviet government's restrictive policies, was Ramadan. But I did not really celebrate Ramadan. Before the 1960s, more people used to celebrate Ramadan; after the 1960s, it was celebrated by fewer people because we were busy then. Today, it seems like more people celebrate Ramadan, including me.

Since we [my generation] lived most of our lives in the Soviet Union, we are kind of russified. We call ourselves Muslims, but a true Muslim should perform the five main rituals of Islam and wear special clothes, but we do not like that lifestyle — we do not want to have long beards and long coats down to our ankles. So, we are unlikely to really turn to Islam. But there is a big possibility that the young generation will turn to Islam. If every Kyrgyz person becomes religious, we will end up, I guess, building a "Caliphate country," like the Islamic countries in the Middle East. Personally, I do not really follow our religion. I perform some of the rituals of Islam, but it's just because I don't want to be separated from the community. But I think we actually follow the traditions of our "true" religion, which is shamanism. We pray to the sun and moon and make birch smoke in our houses.

Although I am not religious, I pray to God often, but I do not follow any religious rules or regulations. I never attended mosque. There was no mosque in the Soviet period and there were no religious schools. I did not start going to mosque even after ndependence, when mosques were built. Throughout my life, I tried to stay away from religion, since I knew what the consequences might be. And besides, all in all, I don't think religions or special places like mosques are necessary in order to communicate with God.

During my childhood, we didn't even have a grocery store so I hadn't seen many different types of food. There wasn't much choice of what to eat: we just ate whatever we had. Many times, I had to eat foods that you would not even consider foods. We had to gather algae and *boburgon* [grasses that grow on the mountains], wash them and eat them. Sometimes we used grind *chie* [a fruit that people normally do not eat], mix it with water, and eat it. I remember, sometimes our mouths used to get inflamed because we were eating all these different wild plants and we would be afraid to eat more, because of the pain they gave us, but we had no other choice — we had to eat to survive.

Even today, there are some foods that I am afraid to eat: the Chinese foods that are spreading rapidly through our region. I have seen people who got ill because they ate Chinese food. That's why I try to avoid eating any foreign foods. For the most part, we grow our food ourselves. That has been a tradition for me since my childhood. My parents used to grow their own food. My favorite food is *beshbarmak* but, unfortunately, now I cannot eat it because I cannot afford it. When I was younger, I used to eat mostly *jarma*,[58] *airan*,[59] *maksym*,[60] and milk. Now we live mostly on tea and bread.

I am kind of a conservative person. I get angry when national values and habits change. Lately, I have noticed that the younger generation has started making *beshbarmak* in a different way. Earlier, the pasta for *beshbarmak* was made by hand. Now people buy factory-made noodles. I liked the old way of making our national food. The new version doesn't taste as good. I am never satisfied when I eat ready-made *beshbarmak*. It seems like the eating habits of the Kyrgyz people are changing as well. But I am not changing my eating habits. I used to eat all my food with my hands, if possible. I still do. I can't taste the food if I don't eat it with my hands.

People rarely drank alcohol in the Soviet era, when life was better. But now people drink more and more, as poverty increases. Nowadays, there is no feast, New Years Eve, or party without alcohol. In addition, people tend to have more parties now than they used to. When I was younger, I used to drink alcohol only when I was earning good money. Now I have quit drinking, for two reasons: first, it is kind of uncomfortable to drink at my age — it is kind of shameful for me to drink; second, I cannot really afford to buy alcohol. One bottle of vodka can cost as much as 100 *som*s. If I were to buy vodka for that price, I would have no money for food. So, because of the social and financial constraints I had to quit drinking.

At this point, I do not really do anything for entertainment. Watching my children and grandchildren have fun is my enter-

---

[58] A porridge made from ground grain and water, slightly fermented.

[59] A slightly fermented dairy beverage with a consistency a bit thicker than kefir, usually made from a mixture of milk and sour cream.

[60] Like *jarma*, but with a thinner consistency, more likely to be treated as a beverage, rather than a food.

tainment. I am kind of a hardworking person. I always find some work to do rather than looking for entertainment. That's the way I was when I was younger, too. Usually, when I was free after work, I used to just do household chores. I remember, when we had money, I used to go to parties with my peers and sometimes I used to visit my relatives. After TV came to our village in 1962, it became one of the main source of entertainment for our community. Before TV, young people used to roam around, take care of animals, and sometimes play *ordo*, *chuko*, or *kok boru*.[61]

My first language is Kyrgyz. That's the language my parents used at home and the language I used at school, at work, at home, and in almost all other aspects of my life. I think you can live without speaking any language except Kyrgyz in Kyrgyzstan; I can communicate with people from other regions in Kyrgyz. But more advanced opportunities are not available to people who speak only Kyrgyz. For instance, if you want to work abroad or start a medium-sized business, you will have to deal with people of other nationalities and you will need Russian. Russian is much more prestigious than Kyrgyz, because it is the language used to communicate among different nationalities. Lately, I have noticed that English and Chinese are becoming more popular. They are prestigious and young people are struggling to learn them to improve their prospects.

I have noticed that the use of the Kyrgyz language has changed over time. In the past, Kyrgyz people used to speak pure Kyrgyz. They would speak using only Kyrgyz words and the right pronunciation. Now I rarely meet people who speak "correct, pure" Kyrgyz. Most young people today use Russian words even when speaking Kyrgyz. It is hard to say they are speaking Kyrgyz because half the words they use are Russian, even though they claim they are speaking Kyrgyz. Even presi-

---

[61] Traditional games played with sheep bones or on horseback.

dent Bakiyev does not speak "pure" Kyrgyz. He often uses Russian words and has a Russian accent.

Besides Kyrgyz, I also speak Russian, Uzbek, Kazakh, Tatar, and Bashkir. I learned these languages while serving in the army and studying in a school for drivers. Russian was the only difficult language to learn. All the rest are Turkic languages so they are similar, so it was not that hard to learn them.

Two of my sons live in the village with me and one them is living and working in Almaty, Kazakhstan. He does not really send money to us, but that's okay. I am happy if he can feed himself. He doesn't have to worry about us — we will survive somehow. Many young Kyrgyz people are living and working in other countries — especially Russia. It's good for our economy. I've heard that the remittances sent by labor migrants add up to one billion dollars. They are feeding their families and their parents. One billion dollars is not a joke, it is a significant part of our overall GDP.

But I think all this is a temporary phenomenon. I think the labor migrants will return to their homeland at some point in their lives. In the meantime, I think they are doing the right thing: they should strive for better lives, but when they have earned enough money to support their families, they should come back home. Nothing equals living in your homeland. Now I am old enough to think about going to the "other" world and I want my corpse to be buried in my homeland.

I understand the young people who are moving from the villages to the city [within Kyrgyzstan]. They are looking for better lives. They hope they can find jobs in Bishkek and earn some money. I don't think there should be any restrictions on internal migration. Everybody is struggling to survive. Why would someone interfere when somebody is trying to survive? To keep the young people in the village we should build entertainment centers, attractions, sport stadiums, gyms, and — most importantly — the government should create jobs.

Unemployment is the main reason that young people are migrating to urban areas.

In the city, there is better access to education and information technology. People live more comfortably, with more opportunities for entertainment, better hospitals, etc. But Kyrgyz who people live in urban areas are more vulnerable to globalization; they are losing their national identity, their national culture. Though the villagers tend to be more "pure" Kyrgyz, their knowledge is really limited, since their lives are tightly connected with farming and breeding animals. Young people in the villages are simple. They are simple people and their understanding of the world is simple. In the cities, the young people are more adapted to world culture. They are more modernized than their rural counterparts. I guess living in a city is better and that's why so many youngsters are moving to cities these days.

33. The Haji

Abdysh Asanov, who is Kyrgyz, was born in 1925 in the semi-nomadic village of Kemer, in the Talas province of Kyrgyzstan. During the collectivization drive, he and the rest of his village moved to Ken-Aral and began a settled life. "I had not even seen Nuska, my future bride, when I decided to marry her. I had simply conspired with her sister-in-law to kidnap her. Since there were no cars at that time, I decided to kidnap her by horse," he recalled. Murat Tuloberdiev interviewed him in Ken-Aral on March 22, 2009.

In the early 1930s, the government seized the lands and animals of the rich people by force and gathered everyone together onto *kolkhozes* [collective farms]. After that, people were allowed to have only a limited number of animals and a few plots of land, where they could grow enough vegetables only to meet the needs of their families. Most of the land was owned by the government and shared among the people. I think collectivization was the right thing to do at that time. It helped to transform our old, nomadic way of life into a more modern way of life.

In my childhood, schools were a new thing. Not all the villages had schools. Teachers were very rare and they were not very well educated. They were just tenth-grade graduates. Even though they were not professional teachers, everyone used to show them a lot of respect and obey them. I studied in my village, Kemer, until the third grade. There were no more grades in our school, so, in order to continue my education, I had to get up at five or six in the morning and walk 10 kilometers to a school in a village called Barak.

I was really enthusiastic about learning. Unfortunately I had to work, too, so I wasn't able to pay much attention to my studies. My favorite subjects were math and history. I liked math class because I learned to count and calculate; I liked history because I learned about myself, about human beings, about our past. At that time, we did not even know what extracurricular activities were. Or, rather, our extracurricular activity was work. I only completed the seventh grade, but later, somehow, I got a certificate saying that I had finished tenth grade.

Being able to read, write, and calculate helped me get a job that not everybody could get. However, later on, many young, well-educated professionals started to appear and the ones — like me — without higher education had to quit working. So I was forced to go to college. I studied in Semipalatinsk, Kazakhstan, because there was no college in Bishkek. After graduating with a specialization in agriculture, I was ready to continue my job.

Now, I am getting older and I have few memories of my classmates and my teachers. None of my teachers are alive anymore and all of my classmates have passed away, except two. And even those two remaining classmates are in bad condition. They cannot even get out of their houses because of health problems. So, I can say I am almost the only remaining representative of my generation from our village.

There was a famine in our village during the war. People had to feed themselves, but the priority was feeding the Soviet army. So the villagers tried to send their best food to the front and they ate whatever was left. Everyone was working for kolkhozi, but they were not getting salaries. My father among them. Since no one had any income, only a limited amount of grain was available to them.

We used to grind the grain with a *jargylchak* [a handmade metal or stone mill] into *talkan*, and use it to make *jarma* or *atala*. There was not even enough wood to cook with, so the young children used to go to meadows and gather *kuurai* [a kind of wild grass with a relatively thick stem] and bushes. Life was really tough during the war. People suffered a lot because of hunger, cold, and a lack of clothing.

Before the war, we didn't know much about the Germans so it's hard to say we even had opinions about them. But during the five years of the war, everybody knew who the Germans were. Even after the war, many people hated them. For me, personally, the Germans seemed like friends, not enemies. Especially after the war, I think, they were really useful to the Kyrgyz people — I mean the ones who were sent to our village forcibly. For instance, the Kyrgyz people did not know how to build houses until they came; we just lived in *boz-ui* [*yurts*]. Probably people hated the Germans because of Hitler's fascist, aggressive policy and the Soviet propaganda.

Some of the nationalities that were living within the Soviet Union were moved from their homelands to Central Asia during and after the war. I heard, back in those days, that some of them had betrayed our motherland and cooperated with Nazi Germany. That's why our internal forced migrants were called "traitors" and the German forced migrants were called "occupiers." In the beginning, it was really difficult for the forced migrants. They did not have food, clothing or shelter. But most of them moved away after few years. I thought Stalin's policy of forced migration was good because, otherwise, some of those people could have cooperated with Nazi Germany. Also, the forced migrants were used for labor, of which there was an extreme shortage in our region at that time.

My marriage to my *kempir* [old wife] was interesting. I had not even seen Nuska, my future bride, when I decided to marry her. I had simply conspired with her sister-in-law to kidnap her. Since there were no cars at that time, I decided to kidnap her by horse. My first attempt to trek 30 kilometers on horseback to kidnap Nuska didn't work out. Later, I went to her family and we arranged our marriage. On the day of the arrangement, I saw Nuska for the first time. I remember when I brought her home, her mother escorted her all the way to our house. She and I led a happy life. We brought up 15 children: eight sons and seven daughters. Most of them studied at universities in Moscow and Leningrad.

After the war, life did not get better right away. Though it was not like during the war, life was still difficult — there were shortages of everything. People used to work for the *kolkhoz* but there was still no question of getting salaries. In most cases people got household items or flour for their work. And most of the work was done by hand; the land was even still plowed by horse. Since I was relatively more educated than most peasants, I worked as an *uchetchik* [foreman]. I used to make sure everyone was doing their work in the fields. Every day, I used to get 50 kilograms of flour from the *kolkhoz* and distribute 1-2 kilograms to every family, according to the number of family members. There were not enough scales, so I used my hands to measure the flour.

I worked for a *kolkhoz* as an *uchetchik* and, later, as a kind of an accountant. Our *kolkhoz* mainly used to grow wheat, clover, and *arpa* [barley]. At that time, there was no agricultural equipment. Most work was done by hand. Later, an organization called MTC was created. They had tractors and combines and kolkhozi used rent tractors and combines from them. Later, our kolkhoz got its own equipment and it was constantly being updated. Especially after the collapse of the Soviet Union, new equipment and technologies appeared that we had never seen before. Using the new equipment and planting new types of crops has increased productivity and the quality of the harvest to an incredible extent.

When Stalin died, it was a major blow for the people. People used to like Stalin and they were really shocked. Many people were crying as if they were saying farewell to one of their loved ones, because they believed the Soviet Union beat the fascists only because of Stalin's strong will, high intelligence, and heroic character. I did not really cry. I thought that if he died then it is the way it should be. On one hand, people were mourning because they had lost their beloved leader. On the other hand, they were panicking: What will happen in the future? What kind of leader will come to power next? Will he be as strong as Stalin, able to lead the state to a good, bright future? All these kinds of questions were in the minds of our villagers. Along with these questions there was fear among our people that the U.S. or West Germany would occupy the Soviet Union.

A couple of years after Stalin died, Khrushchev came to power. I don't really rememberany changes he made except that he decreased the number of horses in the Soviet Union and, as I remember, people started getting their wages in cash.

My favorite food was always *beshbarmak*, which is made of handmade pieces of pasta and plenty of meat. Unfortunately, this traditional Kyrgyz food has been changing over time. In the past, people used to make the pasta by hand, but now they just buy pre-made noodles. I really like the old way of making *beshbarmak*. Modern *beshbarmak* does not taste like real beshbarmak. Also, I have noticed that people's table manners are changing. Kyrgyz people used to eat almost every kind of food with their hands. Now, many people — even me — eat with either a spoon or a fork. Besides *beshbarmak*, I used to enjoy eating dishes made from meat and drinking alcohol from time to time.

As time has passed, my taste has changed a lot. At the moment, my favorite foods are basically milk products. This is probably the result of getting old. Now, I usually eat bread or *jupka*[62] and drink milk. I also enjoy *kaimak*[63] and have quit drinking alcohol. When I was a child, I used to dream about eating *kaimak* but, because there was lack of domestic animals, my family could not afford it. I hated eating potatoes, but I had to eat them because they were one of the few things my family

---

[62] A thin slice of bread, often eaten by older Kyrgyz people, especially during the month of Ramadan.

[63] A kind of a sour cream.

used to grow. Since I lived in a small village I did not even have the chance to trying eating foreign foods, except when I was working with Dungans and I ate with them.

When I was young, there was no question of choosing a religion. All I knew about religion was what my parents told me about Islam. When I grew up, I learned that our government didn't allow religion — it used to teach that there was no God. There were no mosques, no *imam*s; it was really hard to imagine being religious. None of my relatives attended a religious school or anything like that, because there weren't really any religious schools. I was always afraid that I would be fired from my job if I had anything to do with religion. I didn't want to risk pursuing my ancestors' religion. Instead, I lived the way the Communists told me to — I even avoided celebrating Ramadan.

However, deep in my heart I always believed in God and, when restrictions on religion were removed after the 1970s, I began to consider myself a little bit religious. After the Soviet Union collapsed, I turned fully religious. Now we have freedom of religion — or at least freedom to be Muslim. Legally, all religious people are free to practice their faiths, but I see some social pressure on minor religions, especially in rural areas. So, I would call the freedom of religion in Kyrgyzstan, freedom of religion for Muslims. Now Muslims can be open about their faith and even try to convince the government to adopt laws that are based on Islamic principles. Now I believe in God and I perform almost all the Islamic rituals: I read *namaz* [pray], believe in the oneness of Allah, give alms to the poor, and fast every year on Ramadan. I have even completed the Haj. After returning, I financed the construction of a mosque in our village. Soon, I am going to build a new madrassa here, too.

Although many things have changed over the years, my family life has not really changed. We succeeded in building an integrated, strong, and healthy family. In my opinion, in order to build this kind of family, there should be a strong, patriarchal father. There should not be democracy within the family. If there is democracy, the family will disintegrate — there will not be unity among the family members and the children will not listen to their parents. Islam says that man should lead woman, not vice versa. There is also a Kyrgyz proverb: bring up the children properly from early childhood, train your wife from the beginning.

Before the Soviet government was established, women did not really have any voice. They would listen to whatever their husbands said and generally were not allowed to go out. Most of their lives were spent inside their houses. Women could not even argue with their husbands if they did not agree with them.

When the Communist government was established, a new law was passed that stipulated that men and women were equal. After that, women started going to school and even to institutes and universities. They started holding high positions in government. Their role in the family decreased and their role in public life increased. As the role of women in public was increasing, the role of men in public was decreasing and their responsibilities at home were growing. Since the collapse of the Soviet Union, many husbands have started sitting at home, doing housework and taking care of the children, while their wives are working and earning money to support their families.

The changing roles of men and women are clear, but it is hard for me to say how the role of youth in society has changed. To avoid exaggeration, I can only say that the youth of my time were much less educated, but used to show more respect for older people, since they were important sources of information and knowledge. Today's youth are modern and well-educated, but have no respect for old people. However, more young people are going to mosques today than in the past.

After the Soviet government collapsed in the 1990s, the process of privatization began. If collectivization was good during a certain period in history, privatization was even better. But this is only what I think. Many other people seem to regret the dissolution of the *kolkhoz*es. I think these people have not been able to understand capitalism. They did not even understand what was going on when the privatization process started. They rejected privatization and thought they would remain on the *kolkhoz*. Personally, I understood that capitalism was good and embraced the privatization process.

I was born in this village and have lived here all my life. Now I have children who live and work in Bishkek and they send me some money if ask, but I do not really need their money. I am self-sufficient. Since privatization, I have acquired 100 hectares of farming land, plus tractors and combines. Everybody got "shares" from the government, but only a few people became successful, since many didn't have the experience and skill to manage private farms. I am one of the most successful farmers in our village and I think that all problems have solutions if you just look for them. Currently, I do not really see any problems with water supply, equipment, or financing. We feed the land and the land feeds us; the more you invest, the more you get. But the ones who rejected privatization are having major problems. I think that the issue is not that these problems exist, but that some people do not understand capitalism and do not want — or do not know how — to solve these issues.

During my childhood, we did not even think about entertainment. We did not even know what entertainment was. Now many people enjoy going to sanatoriums, resorts, and spas, and the young people have found many types of entertainment: they play football and traditional games such as *kok boru*.[64] As for me, I enjoy going to Susamyr, Sary Chelek, Cholpon Ata, and Issyk-Kul to rest.[65] During my childhood my

---

[64] A traditional competition on horseback.

[65] Susamyr is a valley south of Bishkek. Sary Chelek is an alpine lake. Cholpon Ata is a resort town on the shore of Lake Issyk-Kul, an alpine lake.

hobby was to play *chuko*.⁶⁶ Now I guess my favorite thing to do is to visit people. Everyday there is some occasion in the village and, as one of the elders in the village, I am invited. I also enjoy visiting my children and seeing my grandchildren. Television appeared in my village in 1962 and that has become one of the most popular forms of entertainment here. Before that, youngsters used to like to sit together and drink *kumys* [fermented mare's milk].

My first language is Kyrgyz; this is the language I was brought up with at home. I also speak Russian. I learned it when I was in the army and when I was in college. I have always used Kyrgyz in most aspects of my life, but Russian is also important. I speak Kyrgyz with Kyrgyz-speaking people and Russian with Russian-speaking people. Some say that English is getting more prestigious and some say that we should learn Arabic, especially if we want to understand our religion more deeply.

I think Kyrgyz is sufficient within the boundaries of our country, because I can communicate in Kyrgyz with people from all the other regions of Kyrgyzstan. Unfortunately, though, the use of Kyrgyz has changed during my lifetime: in urban areas, many people now tend to speak Russian and are russified, in terms of culture and mentality. I think that is because the Kyrgyz language was neglected during the Soviet period. Still, I think Kyrgyz is the fastest-growing language in Kyrgyzstan. That is because it is associated with our religion and our culture and it is unlikely that Kyrgyz people will neglect their religion and their native language.

These days, labor migrants have started moving to foreign countries in search of better lives. I think that only works in the short run. Their lives improve, but only temporarily. There is a Kyrgyz proverb: it is better to be a slave at home than to be a governor in a foreign nation. Those who move to foreign coun-

---

⁶⁶ A game similar to marbles, but played with sheep bones.

tries do not have relatives to support them in case of emergency. And it doesn't matter how well they live there, they will have to come back home eventually. They cannot be buried in foreign country; if Kyrgyz people are buried outside of their native land, it is a great shame for our society. If my children were living permanently abroad and asked me to live with them, I would visit, but I wouldn't stay forever. I would rather live in my homeland with my people than live in a foreign country with my children. But I think external migration is good for our economy. Though labor migrants' incomes do not affect our country's budget, they help the people directly, because the migrants send remittances to their parents, families, and relatives.

As far as internal migration is concerned — from villages to cities — I think there should be restrictions. So many villagers are leaving their homes in the search of better lives in the cities that there is shortage of agricultural workers in rural areas and a surplus of laborers in urban areas like Bishkek. The migrants are making life in both the city and in the village worse; it would be better if they would return to their villages. So I think there should be some kind of law prohibiting the migration of villagers to cities.

However, I think this is a temporary phenomena, which will resolve itself. There is still an inflow of villagers into cities, which means the cities must still have the capacity to accept new migrants. But, as this process continues, cities will have massive excess populations. This will mean no jobs or very low salaries and newly arrived, unskilled villagers will not be able to find jobs and will have no choice but to return to their villages. I have already seen quite a few youngsters return to the village, since they were not really successful in finding a better life in the city.

So it seems like the issue has already started solving itself. I think both the city and the village are have pluses and minuses. Living conditions are good in the city. There are cinemas, theaters, and parks. There are apartments with hot and cold water and central gas and heating. There are more chances to use innovative technology and get educated. But you should keep in mind that you will benefit from all these things only if you have money. If you have no money, you will just be discarded. And also, the polluted air and constant noise make people stressed out and unhealthy. On the other hand, in the village, there is clean water, fresh air, and beautiful nature. All the food is healthy because it is produced in our own gardens. And villagers do more physical work, so they are healthier.

Printed in Great Britain
by Amazon